Grammar Done Right!

A clear, commonsense approach to grammar, usage, and style

Revised and Expanded 2nd Edition

Karen L. Reddick

Happy Writing!
Karen Reddick

Disclaimer: This publication is designed to provide accurate and authoritative information regarding the subject matter. The author and/or publisher disclaim any and all liability, directly or indirectly, for advice or information presented herein. The author and/or publisher does not assume any responsibility for errors, omissions, or interpretation of the subject matter herein.

Library of Congress Control Number: 2009901009
2nd Edition
ISBN 13:978-0-9789904-3-5 (pbk.)
ISBN 10: 0-9789904-3-9 (pbk.)

Cover Design and Interior Layout: Ronda Taylor, Taylor by Design

WHAT OTHERS ARE SAYING...

A comprehensive, easy-to-follow grammar and punctuation guide. "As a professional writer, I always think I'm a master at grammar and punctuation, and the truth of the matter is I often have to refer to the experts like Karen to proofread my work. She's absolutely the best, and I should know. I've worked with a lot of editors. I've also purchased many grammar books, and this by far is the easiest one to follow that I've ever used. I can find everything I need quickly and it addresses the questions I personally seem to encounter the most. I highly recommend this book to anyone who needs a comprehensive, easy-to-follow grammar and punctuation guide."

— Rhonda Ryder, CEO, Help Me Rhonda Marketing.com

Guaranteed to save you time. "In stellar fashion, Karen has delivered on her promise of giving—in a clear, commonsense way—explanations and examples of how to write correctly. I found plenty of gems throughout as Karen tackles the essential grammar basics. This book came across my desk when I was questioning several elements for a biography I was editing and it saved me the time and effort of looking them up. I guarantee it will do the same for you!"

— Barbara McNichol, Barbara McNichol Editorial

A great reference tool! "Karen Reddick has been sharing countless valuable and easy-to-understand grammar tips with businesses and individuals for years. And now she has made access to all of this must-have information easier than ever with her *Grammar Done Right!* book. Whether you consider yourself to be an expert member of the "Grammar Police" or you feel nervous and anxious at the mere mention of the word "grammar," this is the book for you. Find what you need quickly and easily – without making the same mistakes or asking the same grammar-related questions you have been making and asking for years. I don't know anyone in business who should not have this great reference tool handy at all times!"

— Allison Nazarian, Get It In Writing, Inc.

"*Grammar Done Right* **is a Field Guide** to help any writer or student improve their knowledge on the essentials of grammar, speech and sentence structure. I have two boys who use this book as a reference point for school projects, reports and homework. It is definitely an educational tool that we can all benefit from. If you're looking for a refresher course in punctuation and grammar then this book will lend itself to reestablishing your writing skills."

— *Michael Timothy, Author,* Healing Reflections for the Soul

"**A Must Have for Authors, Virtual Assistants, Anyone Who Writes.** I have enjoyed Karen's weekly newsletters with grammar tips for ages and eagerly awaited the arrival of this new book. As an author/publicist/virtual assistant, it's critical for me to present the best when I write something. This amazing book fits right beside my computer for quick access and it has everything I need in an easy to find format. It takes me seconds to find answers and best yet, I know I'm correct and that builds confidence in my writing. I truly believe this is a must have book for all authors, virtual assistants, businesses, etc., whether writing a book, or simply sending out a business letter. I was extremely pleased."

— *Diana Ennen, Author, Owner, Virtual Word Publishing*

"**A Great Resource For My Entire Team!** This book has been a great tool several times over since I purchased it. It is very nicely organized and I have yet to run across a question that doesn't have an answer waiting for me in this book. I like my copy so much and use it so often, I bought copies for each of my team members and it is the first resource we all use."

— *Debbie Tester, Owner, Outer-Office, LLC*

"**Clean, Concise, WOW!** I had the pleasure of interviewing Karen Reddick on MODCOM Radio. She spoke about her business and her book, *Grammar Done Right.* But it wasn't until I received my own copy that I realized what a true gem it is! Karen takes everything confusing and lays out the explanations in a clean, concise manner. The side tabs are excellent for quick referencing; the book is a lightweight powerhouse of information any person using the English language needs to have on hand. My copy is already wrinkled and dog-eared, which is a true sign of a great book! Thanks for writing such a great desk reference, Karen!"

— *Melanie O'Kane, Virtual Assistant, Author and BlogTalk Radio Host*

"A handy desk reference and practical guide for the everyday writer. Common grammar questions are clearly explained through examples. Well laid out with easy tabs for quick navigation and easy look up. This will book is a mainstay on my desk."

— Cheryl Callighan, Master Virtual Assistant, Certified Author's Assistant

"A Must Have, Handy Reference! This handy little reference book stays very close to my computer keyboard, for those times when I forget or confuse a pesky grammar rule from my school days. One of the attractions to this book is the no nonsense approach to common grammar problems in everyday writing. This book is easy to navigate with a comprehensive table of contents, index, and printed tabs throughout. It makes a great gift, too!"

— Teri Dempski, Professional Author's Assistant

"This is a must-have resource. Too many times I've wondered if the emails I'm sending are grammatically correct. This book is like having an editor sitting next to you as you write. A quick scan of the book and it's obvious that Karen understands what we all are thinking; "a vs. an," "that vs. who" are only a few examples in the Word Choice section. I will wear out this book in no time at all. "

— Andrea Kalli, Author, Owner, Entrepreneur

To Those Who Love to Write

TABLE OF CONTENTS

INTRODUCTION

During the writing of this 2nd Edition, I was asked to speak at the American Business Women's Association on the topic of "Good Grammar = Good Business." Great topic! I was forced to determine and make clear: Why is grammar so important to good business? Great question!

Well, for one, a misplaced comma or unclear sentence has been known to cost companies millions of dollars. Need another reason? A survey of hiring managers showed that applications with spelling or grammar errors were rarely considered for the job. You already know that first impressions are lasting impressions; good grammar shows a willingness to care about your written image. It's not just about following a bunch of rules, it's about being understood, showing respect, and getting respect.

I've been sharing weekly grammar tips with my subscribers through my e-zine, *Grammar Tips from The Red Pen Editor,* since March 2006. Putting those tips into an easy-to-reference book was inevitable. Hence, the 1st Edition of *Grammar Done Right!* was born. This expanded and revised 2nd edition offers more great tips, while cleaning up some of the missed typos and mistakes found in the 1st edition. My intent in writing this book, like the last, is to give you quick tips on some of the more basic rules of grammar and sensible sentence structure with a few word terms and usage thrown in for good measure.

This book is not intended to be an all-inclusive scholarly treatise on the subject of grammar, but rather a practical, modern reference for the everyday writer. The primary purpose of this book is to help you write better by providing clear, concise, commonsense grammar and style rules.

I welcome and encourage your feedback on how I can make this resource more useful for you. Please email me at Karen@TheRedPenEditor.com.

Happy Writing!

NUMERALS & NUMBERS

NUMERALS & NUMBERS

Numerals or Words?

Several factors play a part in choosing between spelling out numbers or using numerals.

As a general rule (and I use "general" lightly because there are many exceptions and special cases to this rule), spell out the following (except in technical or scientific context):

- whole numbers from one through one hundred
- round numbers (like hundreds, thousands, millions)
- any number beginning a sentence

Whole numbers:

Twenty-two ball players from eleven teams were packed into three vans.
Twenty-two ball players divided 150 sodas between themselves.
That old bridge is three hundred years old.
The two new parking lots will provide space for 320 more cars.
The population of our town now stands at 2,110.

Round numbers:

A millennium is a period of one thousand years.
Some forty-seven thousand persons attended the fair.
The population of our city is more than three hundred thousand.
An estimated twelve million Americans visited Las Vegas last year.

Numbers beginning a sentence:

One hundred ten writers entered the writing contest.
Nineteen thirty-two was marked, among other things, by the Great Depression.

If those sentences look awkward, reword the sentence to read:
In all, 110 writers entered the writing contest.
The year 1932 was marked by . . .

There's also an alternate rule and one you'll see widely used:

Simply remember to spell out only single-digit numbers and use numerals for all others. Except when beginning a sentence.

Examples:

Eight cars crashed on the highway, and all but 16 drivers were injured.

The mailman dropped off 12 packages; six of which were crushed.

Still not sure? Just remember this: If in doubt, spell it out!

Ages

Deciding between using numerals or words for ages is not considered a *grammatical issue,* and there are no "rules" or no right or wrong way to express numerical amounts, it is; however, a *style issue.*

The question of whether to use words or numerals is completely driven by the material. If you are using several references; say, in regards to various age groups of children: 2- to 4-year olds, 3- to 5-year olds, 8- to 10-year olds 10- to 12-year olds, and so on, you would want to use numerals because it would just look odd and be awkward to spell out the ages.

So, in short, there is no rule about numbers, but there are many equally acceptable styling conventions. It all depends on what works for the text at hand.

Examples:

21-year-old hostess

80-year-old grandfather

6-year-old daughter

twenty-one-year-old hostess

eighty-year-old grandfather

six-year-old daughter

IMPORTANT NOTE The hyphen is only used if your numerals act as adjective to the noun, as shown above. No hyphens are used if the numerals do not describe the noun.

Examples:

The hostess was 21 years old.

Her grandfather ran a marathon when he was 80 years old.

Their daughter turned 6 years old today.

Hyphenating Numbers and Numerals

Hyphens are not used when using numbers with an abbreviation.

Examples:

the *44 m* race

a *5 kg* fish

a *4 ft. high* tree

But ARE used when the abbreviation is spelled out.

Examples:

the 44-meter race

the 5-kilogram fish

the 4-foot-high tree

Hyphens are not used with numerals and percentages unless you are writing in the realm of science and technology.

Examples:

25 percent

a *15 percent* pay raise

DO use a hyphen with numbers preceding a noun or describing the noun.

Examples:

fifth-floor apartment

105th-floor view

second-place winner

Use a hyphen with numbers with superlative.

Examples:

second-best choice

fourth-largest city

third-to-last runner

Use a hyphen with numbers spelled out (double digit numbers like, twenty-one through ninety-nine are hyphenated; others are not).

Examples:

forty-eight

five hundred

nineteen fifty-eight

four hundred fifty

Use a hyphen for numbers spelled out with a noun.

Examples:

the *hundred-meter* dash

450-page book

three-inch-high stiletto heels

NOTE: DO NOT use a hyphen if the noun comes before.

Examples:

He finished *third to last*.

Our city is the *fourth largest*.

The apartment is on the *fifth floor*.

Time of Day

We know we set our clock forward one hour in the spring "spring ahead" and set our clocks back one hour in the fall "fall back." But, many people get confused on how the Time of Day is written.

DST is the acronym for Daylight Saving Time. Many people incorrectly refer to this as Daylight "Savings" Time. However, there is no [s] at the end of Saving. In the fall, when DST ends, we move into Daylight Standard Time.

Time zones should be written in capitals and in parentheses.

Examples:

3:30 p.m. (EST) eastern standard time

2:00 p.m. (CDT) central daylight time

10:30 a.m. (MST) mountain standard time

9:15 a.m. (PDT) pacific daylight time

When writing the time of day, the abbreviations for a.m. and p.m. may be set in small capitals (without periods) or as abbreviations (lowercase with periods). Use a space after the time and before the abbreviation.

(NOTE: AM is the Latin term for *ante meridiem,* which means, before noon. PM is the Latin term for *post meridiem,* which means, after noon.)

Examples:

8:30 a.m. or 8:30 AM

10:30 p.m. or 10:30 PM

The abbreviations a.m. and p.m. should not be used with morning, afternoon, evening, night, or o'clock.

Examples:

8:30 a.m. or eight thirty in the morning

10:00 PM or ten o'clock at night

Except in the twenty-four-hour system (used in Europe and in the military), numerals should not be used to express noon or midnight.

Incorrect: The meeting adjourned at 12:00 PM.
Incorrect: The meeting lasted until 12:00 AM.
Correct: The meeting adjourned at noon.
Correct: The meeting lasted until midnight.

Using The En Dash with Inclusive Numbers

Use the en dash between two numbers when you are implying the numbers go up to and including, or through. Do not use the en dash if the word *from* or *between* is used before the first of a pair of numbers. Instead, *from* should be followed by *to* or *through*, and *between* should be followed by *and*.

Inclusive numbers spelled out should not be joined be an en dash.

Using the en dash.

Examples:

Please refer to pages 60–75 in your notebooks.

Enclosed are the figures for 2001–2007.

The children were divided into age groups 5–7, 8–10, 11–13, and 14–16.

Do not use the en dash.

Examples:

Read from 60 to 75 in your notebooks.

The figures are from 2001 to 2007.

Between 150 and 200 people signed up for the program.

From January 1, 2007 to December 31, 2007.

Spelled Out

Examples:

Women aged forty-five to forty-nine years attended the conference.

There were approximately 20 sixty- to seventy-year-olds.

PUNCTUATION

Punctuation

Punctuation

Apostrophes

Apostrophes show possession, indicate a contraction (the omission of one or more letters or numbers), or are used to form the plurals of some letters and abbreviations.

Possession

Use an apostrophe to form a possessive noun or pronoun. Use the apostrophe even when the item in possession is not stated, but is implied.

Examples:

We went to Doug's house for dinner.

We went to Doug's for dinner.

Compound Possessives

We all know that the possessive form of most singular nouns is created by adding an apostrophe and the letter [s] to the end of the noun. Additionally, the possessive of plural nouns (except for a few irregular plurals that do not end in [s]) are created by just adding the apostrophe.

What happens when two nouns are written as one unit? They're called compound possessives.

Closely linked nouns are treated as a single unit when forming the possessive if the entity "possessed" is the same for both nouns; only the second element takes the possessive form.

Examples:

my aunt and uncle's house (The house belongs to the aunt and the uncle.)

the dog and cat's veterinarian (The cat and the dog go to the same doctor.)

Minneapolis and St. Paul's transportation system (The two cities share a transportation system.)

When the entities are different, both nouns take the possessive form.

Examples:

the dog's and cat's special toys (They both have their own toys.)

New York's and Denver's transportation systems (These states can't possibly have the same transportation system, since they are geographically separated.)

our friends' and neighbors' horses (Unless our friends also happen to be our neighbors, different sets of horses are mentioned).

Contractions

Use an apostrophe to denote a contraction. Contractions can be formed from two words or just by purposely leaving out letters. The apostrophe is placed where the missing letters would be.

Examples:

It's a beautiful day

Don't cry over spilled milk

The report was produced in '95

Here's wishin' you luck

Singin' in the rain

There ain't nothin' to it

Rock 'n' roll

Meet'n

Plurals

Use an apostrophe and an [s] to form the plural of lowercase letters, and the capital letters A, I, M, and U. Note: A, I, M, and U are the only capital letters that require an apostrophe to form the plural because, without the apostrophe, adding an [s] would form a different word.

Examples:

A's = As

I's = Is

M's = Ms

U's = Us

Be sure to dot your i's and cross your t's.

The instructor gave few A's in the class.

Punctuation

Use an apostrophe, but do not add an [s], to form the plural of a word that ends in the letter [s].

Examples:

Bridget Jones' Diary is a chick flick.

The virus' genetic code mutates frequently.

Other Uses

Use an apostrophe and an [s] to form the plural of a word used to refer to the word itself.

Example:

Make sure you cover all the if's, and's, and but's.

Use an apostrophe and an [s] to form the plural of an abbreviation that contains periods.

Examples:

The university has many Ph.D.'s on its faculty.

R.N.'s who wish to further their education will like the evening program.

Don't use an apostrophe for numbers, abbreviations without periods, and symbols used as words.

Examples:

7s

1960s

UFOs

VAs

Brackets and Braces

Did you ever wonder why newspapers articles sometimes have brackets [ ] around certain words?

Brackets are used to insert explanations, corrections, clarifications, or comments into quoted material. Brackets are always used in pairs; you must have both an opening and a closing bracket.

Do not confuse brackets with parentheses. Parentheses are used to enclose supplemental information in your own writing; brackets are editorial marks used to insert comments into someone else's words that you are quoting or to insert material into a passage already in parentheses.

Use brackets to indicate you have inserted your own words into a quotation to explain or clarify it. The rules for using punctuation marks with brackets are the same as those for parentheses.

Examples:

Jim said, "She [Julie] finished the report last week."

"No more [government] equipment will be purchased for use in the facility," said Mark.

Place the word sic (meaning "it is so" or "this is the way it was written") in brackets in a quotation to show that an error appeared in the original document. If you want to correct the error, add the correction in brackets.

Examples:

The note said, "telephone [sic] your assistant as soon as you arrive."

The candidate stated, "I grew up in Tuscon [Tucson] in the 1970s."

Use brackets to insert information within parentheses.

Example:

While cleaning my garage, I found clothes I no longer wear (including pants, dresses [formal], and skirts).

Use brackets to insert stage direction into a play.

Example:

[Enter stage left]

Braces { }, on the other hand, are used to group items or to show a relationship among lines, symbols, or formulas in mathematical, statistical, or chemical equations.

Bulleted Lists

Bulleted lists are itemized, targeted points that are written as supporting facts to emphasize your main idea. They are used to bring attention to your idea and are set apart from the main body of text to visually appeal to your reader. They are also used to give examples, for sequencing, or to show benefits of a determined subject.

So what's the rule for using capitalization and punctuation when creating bullet lists?

When using bulleted lists, punctuation and capitalization is not needed if the bulleted point is not a complete sentence.

Example:

For our next scheduled meeting you will need to bring:

- the company employee manual
- your calendar
- your written goals
- a plan of action
- an open mind

Use caps and punctuation if the list is a complete sentence:

Example:

When you join our book club your membership includes these benefits:

- Members receive discounts on featured books signed by the author.
- Registration fees are waived for monthly seminars.
- Membership cards are recognized by major book retailers with a 20% discount.
- The monthly newsletter, mailed directly to your doorstep.

If the order or sequencing of your points is important, use either numerical or alphabetical bullets.

Example:

These are the five steps to success when taking a written exam:

1. read all directions
2. read the questions to be answered
3. underline or highlight important text
4. re-read the question
5. answer the question

Another tip when using bullets is to keep your points consistent. Don't use some with punctuation and some without in the same list.

Capitals in Headlines or Articles

What's the correct way to use capitalization in headline or article titles?

Always capitalize the first and last words both in titles and in subtitles and all other major words (nouns, pronouns, verbs, adjectives, adverbs, and some conjunctions).

Lowercase the articles: *the, a,* and *an.*
Lowercase prepositions, regardless of length, except when they are stressed (i.e., *through* in *A River Runs Through It*).

Or, when used as adverbs or adjectives:
up in *Look Up*
down in *Turn Down*
on in *The On Button*

Lowercase the conjunctions: *and, but, for, or, nor.*
Lowercase the words: *to* and *as* just for simplicity's sake.

Examples:

A Little Learning Is a Dangerous Thing

Singing While You Work

Tired but Happy

Taking Down Names, Spelling Them Out, and Typing Them Up

Sitting on the Floor in an Empty Room

Turn On, Tune In, and Enjoy

Capitalizing Kinship Names

When should you capitalize the names of relatives when used as titles?

Kinship names are lowercased unless they immediately precede a personal name or are used alone, in place of a personal name. What about terms of endearment? They are always lower case.

Examples:

The Gardener brothers run a lawn maintenance business.
We're meeting Uncle Bill for dinner.
I think Grandmother's maiden name was Jackson.
I saw Dad leaving for work.
Come on, honey, let's go.

Some exceptions:

My father and mother fly in tonight. (lowercase after a pronoun)
She loves her aunt, Mabel. (lowercase when used as a descriptive tag)

Capitalizing Popular Names

Popular names of places are usually capitalized. Quotation marks are not needed (unless the word is used with an epithet—see page 18. Always use popular names in a context where they will be easily understood by your reader.

Examples:

the Bay Area
the Beltway
the Cape
the Gaza Strip
the Gulf
Silicon Valley
Skid Row
the Upper West Side
the Wild West
the Windy City

If the term is considered political rather than geographical, terms are lowercased.

Examples:

the iron curtain

the third world

Capitalize a generic part of an urban area if it is adjacent to a specific city, town, county, or state.

Example:

New York's Business District

Capitalize the word *greater* when using it with the name of a city, denoting an entire metropolitan area.

Example:

Greater Chicago

Greater London

Academic Titles

Academic titles are often written incorrectly, even when the author's desire is to show the utmost respect to the educated person.

For example:

Dr. Ima Smartie, Ph.D.

This double title is considered redundant and should not be used both before and after the name.

The above example can be correctly written in several different forms. When using a degree acronym, BA, MA, MBA, following a person's name, the use of periods is optional; the use of capitals is not, but do remember to use the comma after the name.

Examples:

Professor Smartie

Dr. Ima Smartie

Ima Smartie, PhD

Ima Smartie, Ph.D.

The use of Dr. should be reserved for use to refer to someone in the medical profession, be it veterinary, dental, or other medical specialty.

It is not uncommon for people to incorrectly refer to professors as *Dr.* when they mean *professor,* unless the professor holds a doctorate degree (i.e., Doctor of Philosophy or Ph.D.).

There is an academic standard for referring to a person's degree rank. Capitalize these formal titles if written before the name.

Examples:

Professor Smartie

Assistant Professor Smartie

This rule changes when using the title after the name.

Example:

Ima Smartie, professor of philosophy

When writing the title out, do not use capitals or an apostrophe, however, if specifying the degree, the use of the apostrophe is mandated.

Examples:

Ima Smartie, bachelor of arts

Ima Smartie holds a master's in business administration

Epithets (Nicknames)

An epithet is a term used as a descriptive substitute to characterize the name or title of a person or thing. Always capitalize epithets.

Examples:

Catherine the Great

Babe Ruth

Ivan the Terrible

the Swedish Nightingale

Stonewall Jackson

Enclose the epithet in quotation marks and place it inside the name or immediately after it when it is used in addition to a name. No parentheses are necessary.

Examples:

George Herman "Babe" Ruth

Ivan IV, "the Terrible"

Jenny Lind, "the Swedish Nightingale"

Capitalize epithets when they are used as the name of characters in fiction or drama.

Examples:

Dorothy encountered the Tin Man and the Cowardly Lion.

John Barrymore performed brilliantly as Chief Executioner.

Commas

Between Parts of a Sentence

Use a comma before the following conjunctions (for, and, nor, but, or, yet, so) if the conjunction joins two complete, independent statements. (Meaning each statement has a subject and a verb.) HINT: Need an easy way to remember these conjunctions? They spell *FANBOYS*.

Example:

She plans to work all summer, and she will save the money she makes.

DO NOT use a comma unless both of the statements are complete and independent.

Example:

She plans to work all summer and save the money she makes.

DO NOT use a comma to separate two complete statements with a *FANBOYS* conjunction if the sentence has an introductory word or phrase that applies to both statements.

Example:

Please take out the garbage and empty the dishwasher.

Between Two Words

Use a comma between two adjectives ONLY if you can reverse the adjectives and the sentence still makes sense. DO NOT use a comma if the adjectives cannot be reversed.

Examples:

The talkative, noisy group was asked to leave the meeting.

I went to a tough high school.

Use a comma to separate two identical verbs next to each other in a sentence.

Example:

Whatever happens, happens.

Use a comma to separate words repeated for emphasis.

Example:

This project took a long, long time to complete.

Before and After Nonessential Information

Use a comma before and after words or phrases that are not essential to the main idea of the sentence. Meaning, you can remove the word or phrase and the sentence will still make sense.

Examples:

Needless to say, I am going to be late.

Most people, on the other hand, will be on time for the meeting.

The magazine, issued in June 1992, sold more copies than any other magazine in history.

Use a comma to set off words that are not essential and interrupt the natural flow of a sentence. Here are some to look for:

accordingly	unfortunately	by the way
after all	as a rule	for example
however	of course	therefore
in the meantime	also	finally

Commas in a Series

Use a comma to separate a series of three or more equal words, phrases, or complete statements. There's argument surrounding this rule that the third comma is not necessary. In formal writing leave it in. In informal writing you can be more relaxed, but just be sure to stay consistent.

Examples:

You need a saddle, stirrups, and reins to ride a horse.

I wrote the proposal, Susan typed it, and Mike presented it.

I went to the post office, bought groceries, and picked up my daughter from school.

DO NOT use a comma if you join the series with *and*.

Example:

You need a saddle *and* stirrups *and* reins to ride a horse.

DO NOT use a comma before an ampersand (&) in an organization name, unless the comma is used by the organization.

Example:

Tom hired the law firm of Smith, Jones & Brown.

Dashes

What the heck is an en and em dash? How am I supposed to use it?

Dashes are used to show a range, or in place of, parentheses to show that information has been inserted into a sentence.

I find there's an overuse of the dash, and believe the dashes should only be used in informal writing. Use parentheses, commas, or colons for academic and business writing.

IMPORTANT: Dashes do not have spaces before or after.

En Dash (–)

An en dash is the shorter dash symbol. (Printers named the en dash because its length is that of the letter "n.") Use an en dash to show a range of dates, numbers or locations. In all uses of the en dash you should be able to substitute the word *to* or *through* for the dash.

Examples:

The report covers the period 1998–1999.

Please read pages 70–77 in your text.

The Denver–Las Vegas flight is on time.

Em Dash (-- or —)

The em dash is the longer symbol, or as shown here, two hyphens. (The em dash was named because it has the same length as the letter "m.") Use an em dash to indicate an interruption or an abrupt change in thought or to insert supplemental information. If the interruption or insertion comes in the middle of a sentence, use a closing dash to signal the end of the interruption.

Examples:

Last week—I think it was Monday—the manuscript was published and sent to the printer.

Faith, hope, and love—these virtues are important in life.

A solid-colored top—such as the black sweater, the brown vest, or the red shirt—would probably look best with those pants.

Ellipsis

An ellipsis is a set of three periods that indicates the omission of words from quoted material, hesitation, or trailing off in dialogue or train of thought. IMPORTANT: An ellipsis should have spaces before, between, and after the periods. [. . .]

With quoted material, use an ellipsis to indicate an omission at the beginning, within, or at the end of a sentence. When the omission is at the end of a sentence you must first insert the appropriate punctuation to end the sentence (a period, a question mark, or an exclamation mark) and then add the ellipsis.

Examples:

Tom finished his remark, " . . . and I will not arrive until 5:15 p.m."

Michael asked, "Will we leave in the morning? . . . What should I bring?"

Susan cried, "Help! . . . I've fallen and I can't get up!"

Use an ellipsis in fictional writing to indicate hesitation or trailing off in dialogue or train of thought. If the sentence is considered incomplete, use only the ellipsis. If the sentence is considered complete, use a period and the ellipsis.

Examples:

We were lost in the dark forest . . . could that be . . . yes, a light up ahead!

Shannon was not sure she wanted to go . . .   OR

Shannon was not sure she wanted to go. . . .

Hyphens (Dashes)

Before and After for Compound Words

What's your hyphen doing? There are many rules and exceptions to the rules for the hyphen. One of the hardest things to figure out with hyphens is how to use them in two-word descriptions. When two words are combined to describe a noun, sometimes you use a hyphen between them and sometimes you don't.

The first question to ask is whether the description comes before or after the noun.

If it's after the noun, don't use a hyphen.

Examples:

My daughter [noun] is strong willed.

My sister [noun] is red haired.

This burger [noun] is well done.

If it's before the noun, use a hyphen when either of the two words in the description wouldn't make much sense by itself.

Examples:

She's a strong-willed daughter [noun].

I have a red-haired sister [noun].

This is a well-done burger [noun].

Hyphens are used to join two or more words that act as a single term, to form some compound words, to join some prefixes, suffixes, and to divide words into syllables.

There are, however, a lot of "do not" rules we should be aware of too. Let's look at a few examples of the dos and don'ts:

Use a hyphen to join two or more words that precede a noun and act as one descriptive term (compound adjective).

Examples:

She is a stay-at-home mom.

Stephen King is a well-known author.

Use a hyphen when two or more words act as a single noun or verb, but be careful, some of these compound words can be one word (download), some are two words (voice mail), and some are hyphenated (sister-in-law). Check a current dictionary if you are not certain. A free, online dictionary can be found at www.dictionary.com.

Use a hyphen when a term acts as one word.

Example:

The postmen work all-night shifts. (They work the entire night. The words *all* and *night* act as one term).

Use a hyphen to separate two colors.

Example:

The ocean was filled with a school of blue-green fish.

Use a hyphen after the prefixes *ex, self,* and *all.*

Examples:

My ex-husband's name was Bill.

Self-respect is an important trait to have in life.

The psychic claimed to be all-knowing and all-seeing.

Use a hyphen to avoid doubling a letter.

Example:

All part-time employees must work this weekend.

Use a hyphen to add a capital letter prefix to a word.

Example:

My child is not allowed to see R-rated movies.

DO NOT use a hyphen if the description follows the noun.

Example:

The author was very well known.

DO NOT use a hyphen if you add a figure or capital letter after the main word.

Example:

Did you take your Vitamin E capsule this morning?

DO NOT use a hyphen after the prefixes *dis, pre, re, post,* and *non,* unless the word could be misinterpreted without it or the main word is a proper noun.

Examples:

I recovered my ottoman. (I regained possession of it.)

I re-covered my ottoman. (I put another cover on it.)

DO NOT use a hyphen with adverbs ending in *ly.*

Example:

Tickets for the highly acclaimed movie are now available at the box office.

Exceptions to the "Before and After" Rule for Compound Words

Here are some exceptions to the "before and after" rule for hyphens in two-word descriptions.

If self or quasi is one of the words, always use a hyphen.

Example:

Robert is self-effacing; still, he's a self-confident person. He's our quasi-official leader; the position is only quasi-legal.

If both words could be used separately and still make sense, don't use a hyphen even if they come before a noun.

Examples:

Fluffy is a naughty old cat.
Sunshine is a sweet young pony.

If *very* is one of the two words, forget the hyphen.

Example:

That Monet is a very expensive painting.

If the word *very* is added to a description that would ordinarily take a hyphen (much-admired writer, for example), drop the hyphen.

Example:

She is a very much admired writer.

If one of the two words ends in *ly*, you almost never need a hyphen.

Example:

That's a radically different haircut. It gives you an entirely new look.

If one of the words is *most, least,* or *less,* leave out the hyphen.

Example:

The least likely choice, and the less costly one, is the most ridiculous hat I've ever seen.

Beginnings and Endings

Many of us aren't sure when to use a hyphen at the beginning or ending of a word. Here are some common beginnings and endings that don't usually need a hyphen.

Beginnings:

anti: That entire group was antiwar.

bi: The paychecks come out bimonthly.

co: Her book used many coauthors.

extra: The student's extracurricular schedule is full.

inter: Those two words are interchangeable.

micro, mini or multi: The boss's micromanagement of the project caused a minicrisis among his multitalented staff.

mid: The project lost steam midstream.

non: Susan chose to be nonpartisan in this election.

over and under: It's important to be overcautious if serving alcohol when underage children are present.

post: He came from the postwar era.

semi: He drove that huge semitrailer under that tiny bridge.

sub and super: Our subbasement got supersaturated during the flood.

[Notice the exception here: earlier I stated use a hyphen with double consonants; not the case when using *sub*.]

Endings:

ache: I'll trade a headache for a toothache any day.

less or more: The ageless soprano can still hit the uppermost notes.

like: That painting was so lifelike.

wide: Sewer rats are a citywide problem in some parts of the country.

One Word? Two Words? Or Hyphenated?

One of the issues many writers come up against is whether a two-word phrase is two separate words, hyphenated, or a compound word. I can't find a hard and fast rule for this, but have found that if the word is a noun, it will *usually* be two words. That same word written as a compound noun, adjective, verb, or verb phrase can be either hyphenated, one word, or two words.

Examples:

common sense [noun]	commonsense [adjective]
double cross [noun]	double-cross [verb]
dead end [noun]	dead-end [adjective]
front line [noun]	frontline [adjective]
short circuit [noun]	short-circuit [verb]
Web based [noun]	Web-based [adjective]
backup [compound noun]	backup [adjective] back up [verb phrase]
follow-up [compound noun]	follow up [verb phrase]
knockout [compound noun]	knock out [verb phrase]
rundown [compound noun]	run-down [adjective] run down [verb phrase]

Keep in mind that the English language is fluid and alive. After two words are used together for a time, becoming a part of everyday language, they become hyphenated. Sometimes the hyphenation goes away and the word becomes compound. Check the dictionary for the current usage for a given word/words.

Italics

Drawing a line under a word or phrase indicates the language has been singled out for a specific reason. When you underline, draw one continuous line with no spaces between words. Placing a word in italics is equivalent to underlining it. Did you know that underlining was used by printers and typists because it was easier? Italics have become more common with the advent of the word processor.

Titles

Underline or use italics for the titles of books, magazines, journals, newspapers, and pamphlets. EXCEPTIONS: The Bible, the Koran, legal documents, and their parts are generally not underlined.

Examples:

Did you read John Grisham's *The Painted House*?

Did you see Steve Martin's play *Picasso at the Lapin Agile*?

DO NOT underline or italicize the punctuation marks except in abbreviations.

Underline or use italics for the titles of movies, videos, plays, television and radio programs, operas, long poems, long musical works, works of art, and published speeches.

Examples:

Saving Private Ryan was a very popular movie.

Lincoln's *Gettysburg Address* is one of the most moving speeches of all time.

The *Mona Lisa* hangs in the Louvre in Paris.

Proper Names

Underline or use italics for the names of ships, trains, aircraft, and spacecraft.

Example:

The aircraft carrier *U.S.S. Enterprise* is one of the largest ships afloat.

Foreign Words

Underline or use italics for scientific names, foreign words or phrases, and the names of legal cases. Note: The *v* in legal cases (Latin for versus or against) appears in regular font style in a legal citation.

Examples:

canis lupus

Semper fidelis

Roberts v. *Davis*

Words Being Used as Examples

Underline or place in italics words being defined or words, letters, or numbers being named as words or used as examples.

Example:

The letters *ch* can be pronounced like *sh*, as in the word *chic*.

DO NOT underline for emphasis; instead, choose stronger words.

Example:

The girl was <u>pretty</u>.

The girl was beautiful.

Percentages

When writing percentages, do we spell out the number or use the % sign, or spell out the word percent or write in numerals?

In general writing, the percentage number is almost always expressed as a figure. Except when used at the beginning of a sentence.

Examples:

Only 15 percent of the board members voted.

With 90–95 percent of the manuscript completed, the book is almost done.

Twenty-five percent of the employees caught the flu.

In technical writing and in tables and footnotes, percentages are styled as figures plus the percent sign (%).

Examples:

Only 10% of the mice were observed to react to the stimulus.

The treatment resulted in a 20%–25% reduction in discomfort.

NOTE: No space appears between the numeral and the % sign.

The word *percentage* or *percent* when used as a noun without an adjacent numeral, should never be replaced by a percent sign.

Punctuation

Examples:

Only a small percentage of the mice exhibited a growth change.

The clinic treated a greater percentage of outpatients this year.

One percent is a very small percentage.

Punctuation within Parentheses and Quotation Marks

The use of punctuation with parentheses and quotation marks can seem pretty confusing. There is no secret or trick; just try to remember the hard and fast rule is: parentheses out, quotations in.

Of course there are always exceptions, which I'll show you below.

Here are a few examples of punctuating with parentheses and quotations. Notice carefully where periods, commas, question marks, and exclamation marks belong.

Parentheses

Rule: The writer's conference was great (except for lunch).

Exceptions:

[When the aside is a separate sentence]

The writer's conference was great! (Although lunch was cold.)

[When the aside is a question or exclamation within the sentence]

The writer's conference was great (was your food cold?); but I didn't care for the lunch.

Quotations

Rule: At the writer's conference, Susan asked me, "Is your food cold?"

Exceptions:

[With a colon]

There are two reasons she hates the nickname "sugar": It's fattening and it's sweet.

[With semicolons]

Susan's favorite song is "My Humps"; she dances to it all the time.

[When the quote stands alone]

Have you seen the show, "The Apprentice"?

[With parentheses]

Donald always has the last word ("You're Fired!").

Italics, Capitals, and Quotation Marks for Emphasis

Good writers choose commanding words in their sentences and only use italics, capitals, and quotation marks when required by punctuation rules. Good writers do not need external emphasis such as italics, capitals, and quotation marks, because good words have intrinsic power. Don't overuse these forms of punctuation or your writing will lose its force (and annoy people because it is more difficult to read).

Italics for emphasis

Examples:

Employees must notify the HR office in writing of *any* absences.

Will I *ever* finish this chapter?

I only *tried* to help!

Capital for emphasis

Examples:

"OK, I'm a Bad Mother," admitted Doris

Manuscripts sent without self-addressed, stamped envelopes WILL BE RETURNED UNREAD.

Scalpers mingled in the noisy crowd yelling, "TICKETS, SIXTY DOLLARS!"

Quotation marks used for emphasis (in a skeptical or sarcastic way):

Example:

Bob's regular Friday night "volunteer work" turned out to be a poker game.

Punctuating Terms of Technology

With the advances in technology, it's hard to determine and understand the correct spelling of terms such as: Internet vs. internet. Is it email, Email or e-mail? Tele-class or teleclass? Web site, web site or website?

Words historically follow a progression as they enter common use in language. At first two words used to describe a term remains two words (i.e., *e-mail* was originally called *electronic mail*). And then the hyphen was added to create electronic-mail. The progression continued and the word electronic was shortened to just the letter *e* creating *e-mail*.

After extensive online research into the correct usage of these terms, I've come to determine that there are many varying opinions. It's no wonder we can't decide what is correct!

But, if you want to be grammatically correct as defined by the Chicago Style Manual (which is considered "The Book" for grammar and style), no one could argue and you'd be correct by using the following terms:

e-mail
e-book
tele-class
Web site
Internet
URL

However, in casual writing, I believe that as long as you stay consistent you can be more relaxed and use the terms below as often shown:

email
ebook
teleclass
website

Semicolon

The semicolon is used in ways similar to that of the period and comma. Because of these similarities, the semicolon is often thought of as a weak period or a strong comma, though its function is usually closer to that of a period.

A semicolon separates independent clauses that are joined together in one sentence without a coordinating conjunction.

Examples:

He hemmed and hawed for over an hour; he couldn't make up his mind.

Cream the shortening and sugar; add the eggs and beat well.

The river rose and overflowed its banks; roads became flooded and impassable; freshly plowed fields disappeared from sight.

Use a semicolon for potentially confusing sentences including those with other commas in them or with particularly long clauses.

Examples:

We fear that this situation may, in fact, occur; but we don't know when.

In a society that seeks to promote social goals, government will play a powerful role; and taxation, once simply a means of raising money, becomes, in addition, a way of furthering those goals.

A semicolon joins two clauses when the second begins with a conjunctive adverb (*furthermore, hence, however, indeed, likewise, moreover, namely, otherwise, therefore*, and *thus* just to name a few).

Examples:

Most people are covered by insurance of one kind or another; indeed, many people don't even see their medical bills.

It won't be easy to sort out the facts of this confusing situation; however, a decision must be made.

A semicolon is used in place of a comma to separate phrases in a series when the phrases themselves contain commas. A comma may replace the semicolon before the last item in a series if the last item is introduced with a conjunction.

Examples:

She flung open the door; raced up the stairs, taking them two at a time; locked herself in the bathroom; and, holding her sides, started to laugh uncontrollably.

We studied mathematics and geography in the morning; English, French, and Spanish right after lunch, and science in the late afternoon.

BONUS: A semicolon is placed outside quotation marks and parentheses.

Examples:

They referred to each other as "Mother" and "Father"; they were considered the typical happily married elderly couple.

She accepted the situation with a smile (but held secret regrets); however, all of that changed when she saw him the next day.

Spaces After Punctuation

Should we use one or two spaces after a period and other punctuation marks?

Did you know that word processors now allow us to do what professional typesetters have been doing for centuries? Consequently, many of the rules we learned as typists (for those of us that used to use mechanical or electric typewriters) do not apply in the world of word processing.

Here are a few rules of typography (word processing) that differ from those we learned to use for the typewriter:

1) Use one space after all punctuation, including periods, question marks, exclamation points, and colons.

   Putting two spaces after these marks of punctuation is a convention that evolved because typewriters were equipped with only monospaced fonts, which made it difficult to see where sentences ended. Word processing creates proportionally spaced fonts, which do not require the extra spaces in order for a series of sentences to be readable.

2) Use typographer's quotation marks.

   Typographer's quotes—the turned, or *curly* quotation marks—are actually quite different from straight quotes, which were all that our old typewriters could muster. (Tip: Turn on *smart quotes* in Microsoft Word to have the curly quotes automatically appear.)

   Straight quotes should be used only as symbols to denote minutes, seconds, feet, and inches—and then, only in charts, tables, and the like.

3) Avoid using the space bar to indent a paragraph or to move text (for example, to center it).

Word processing software offers a host of formatting options including: tab options, centering, right and left justification, and columns. When you use manual spacing rather than formatting the text using these handy functions, you create two problems: your text will never be evenly aligned, and your work will be made more difficult if you ever want to revise the text in any way.

Quotation Marks

When using quotation marks watch for excessive and/or incorrect use of the quotation mark.

Use quotation marks to enclose what someone says (also known as a direct quote).

Example:

Susan said, "Could you buy me a Coke," and John replied, "I'd be happy to."

DO NOT use quotation marks with indirect quotations.

Example:

Incorrect: Susan said that she, "wants John to buy her a Coke." [I'm telling you about what Susan said, but I'm not using her exact words.]

Correct: Susan said that she wants John to buy her a Coke.

If the quotation is half-direct and half-indirect, don't use quotation marks unless you want to emphasize the quotation.

Example:

Incorrect: The newspaper called Mike, "The hero of the game."

Correct: The newspaper called Mike the hero of the game.

Also Correct: The newspaper called Mike "the hero of the game." [Notice there is no comma and *the* is not capitalized.]

What about words or ideas not spoken out loud? In other words, thoughts or questions in someone's mind? They DO NOT need quotation marks.

Example:

Incorrect: "Can I speak in front of this large audience?" Bob wondered.

Correct: Can I speak in front of this large audience? Bob wondered.

Better: Bob wondered, can I speak in front of this large audience.

And finally, use quotation marks to suggest doubt or skepticism.

Examples:

You call this a "car?" I call it a rusty bucket of metal on wheels.

His boss said he did "okay" on his performance review—whatever that means.

Virgule

The virgule (/) is known by many names, including *diagonal, solidus, oblique, slant, slash, forward slash,* and *slash mark.* The virgule is used to represent a word that is not written out or to separate or set off certain adjacent elements of text.

A slash most commonly signifies alternatives. In certain contexts it represents the word *or.*

Examples:

he/she

his/her

oral/written tests

and/or

alumni/ae

A slash represents the word *per* or *to* when used with units of measure or when used to indicate the terms of a ratio.

Examples:

40,000 tons/year

14 gm/100 cc

9 ft./sec.

a 50/50 split

A slash replaces the word *and* in some compound terms.

Examples:

in the May/June issue

1973/74

parent/child problems

A slash punctuates some abbreviations and in lieu of a period.

Examples:

c/o

w/

w/o

S/Sgt

d/b/a

GRAMMAR

Grammar

Adverbs

An adverb is a word that qualifies, limits, describes, or modifies a verb, an adjective, or another adverb. You'll be able to recognize most adverbs because they usually end in [ly].

Examples:

She studied constantly [*constantly* qualifies the verb *studied*]

The juggler's act was really unusual [*really* qualifies the adjective *unusual*]

The cyclist pedaled very swiftly [*very* qualifies the adverb *swiftly*]

Many professional editors and great writers agree that most adverbs are unnecessary and should be cut out whenever possible. They clutter your sentence and annoy the reader. If you choose a strong verb that has a specific meaning, the adverb is redundant.

Examples:

The radio blared loudly [blare connotes loudness]

The father clenched his teeth tightly [there's no other way to clench teeth]

I'm not saying you should never use an adverb, they do have their place, so let's determine the correct position of the adverb when we do use them.

To avoid miscues, the adverb should generally be placed as near as possible to the word it is intended to modify.

Example:

The marathoners submitted their applications to compete immediately. [What does *immediately* modify—*compete* or *submitted?*]

Placing the adverb with the word it modifies makes the meaning clear.

Example:

The marathoners *immediately* submitted their applications to compete.

A misplaced adverb can also completely change a sentence's meaning.

Example:

We *nearly* lost all our camping equipment. [This states that the equipment was saved.]

We lost *nearly* all our camping equipment. [This states that almost everything was lost.]

Misusing adverbs is something I've been guilty of in writing.

Hopefully, happily, sadly, honestly, frankly, and seriously are all adverbs that should be used to describe a verb, because that's what adverbs do, and should not be used to begin a sentence describing our own attitude toward the statement that follows.

Incorrect: Hopefully, the bus will come soon.
Correct: I hope the bus will come soon.

Incorrect: Frankly, his mannerisms disgust me.
Correct: I'm being frank when I say his mannerisms disgust me.

Incorrect: Sadly, somebody else won the lottery this week.
Correct: I'm sad to say that somebody else won the lottery this week.

Incorrect: Honestly, I'm not sure I care.
Correct: In all honesty, I'm not sure I care.

Adjectives

Adjectives add color and precision to our speech. They give life to the objects and ideas named by describing them. Adjectives clarify what we are talking about by enhancing and limiting the designation of a noun or pronoun.

Dates as Adjectives

Dates are often used as descriptive adjectives. Here are a few punctuation and use rules to remember when using dates as adjectives.

If a month-and-day or month-and-year date is used as an adjective, DO NOT use a hyphen or comma.

Examples:

The October 31 Halloween festival promises to be fun for all the kids.

We'll always remember Susan's March 11 birthday party.

The June 2007 financial statement is scheduled for release soon.

Ever since Tom's June 2001 wedding, he has been unable to go out with the boys.

If a full month-day-year date is used, then a comma is necessary both before and after the year.

Example:

The June 4, 2007, commencement ceremonies will take place in the gymnasium.

Even Better:

Commencement ceremonies will take place on June 4, 2007, in the gymnasium.

Order of Adjectives

We are all familiar with using more than one adjective to modify a noun; for example: He's a silly old fool, or she's a smart, independent woman.

When you use more than one adjective to modify a noun, they should be put in a certain order according to type. Use a comma to separate adjectives of **evaluation** (regarded as coordinate adjectives), which means their order can be reversed and the word *and* can be inserted between them. But no commas are used to separate adjectives in other categories.

If you're confused, follow these guidelines to help determine how to order your adjectives.

Determiner: *a, an, the, this, that, these, those,* possessives (*its, our*), quantity words (*many, some*), numerals (*five, nineteen*)

Evaluation or Opinion: *interesting, delicious, comfortable, inexpensive, heavy*

Size: *big, little, huge*

Shape: *round, square, long*

Age: *old, young, new*

Color: *white, red, green*

National Origin: *Italian, European, Asian*

Religious Faith: *Catholic, Buddhist, Mormon*

Material: *oak, ivory, wooden*

A noun used as an adjective: *kitchen* cabinet, *writing* desk

Examples:

Many little white glass buttons

Her beautiful long kitchen table

A delicious, inexpensive Italian meal

Her efficient, hardworking, ambitious virtual assistant

You'll note above that the comma is only used when the adjectives are evaluative adjectives; where we can insert *and* between the adjectives and the order can be reversed.

Examples:

A delicious *and* inexpensive Italian meal

An inexpensive *and* delicious Italian meal

Her efficient *and* hardworking *and* ambitious virtual assistant

Her ambitious *and* efficient *and* hardworking virtual assistant.

Clauses

Let's find out more about the fun world of sentences, specifically, their parts. You may ask why you need to know all of this. If writing is your passion, then having a solid knowledge of what makes a sentence work and what doesn't will separate your writing from the rest.

Different Types of Clauses

Sentences may contain these different types of clauses:

Phrase

A phrase is a group of words that lacks a subject, a verb, or both. Phrases cannot stand alone; they add information to the sentence.

> **Examples:**
> to the store
> in a hurry
> past the window

Independent Clause

An independent clause is a group of words that contains a subject and a verb and can stand alone as a complete sentence.

> **Examples:**
> The designer created the Web site.
> We found a lost dog on our doorstep.

Dependent Clause

A dependent clause is a group of words that consists of a subject and a verb but depends on another clause to complete the thought. A dependent clause begins with a connector (or subordinator); if, when, because, although, since, which, or that and prevents the sentence from standing alone.

> **Examples:**
> because I was late
> when they arrived
> since we're here

Conjunctions

A conjunction joins words, phrases, clauses, or sentences. I think we all know the most common conjunctions and when to use them; and, but, for, or, yet, and so. But here are two conjunctions that always confuse people.

When should you use or and when should you use nor?

Don't let these guys trick you. Remember this simple rule and you'll never be confused again.

When using the word either, use or. They both start with vowels. When using the word neither, use nor. They both start with "n."

Examples:

We had to decide if we were going to either the movies or to dinner.

My boss had neither the time nor the patience to listen to Bill's complaining.

Beginning a Sentence with a Conjunction

Just as there is widespread belief that you should not end a sentence with a preposition, there is also no historical or grammatical foundation that you should not begin a sentence with a coordinating conjunction.

A coordinating conjunction you'll remember is for, and, nor, but, or, yet, so. Once again, I could find no substantiated evidence that beginning a sentence with a conjunction is an error and is mainly taught to avoid writing fragmented sentences.

If you decide to begin a sentence with a coordinating conjunction, keep these points in mind:

- Be sure that a main clause follows the coordinating conjunction.
- Use a coordinating conjunction only when it makes the flow of your ideas more effective.
- Do not use a comma after the coordinating conjunction. Coordinating conjunctions are not considered transitional expressions like in addition or for instance.
- *But* used as an adversative conjunction can sometimes be unclear at the beginning of a sentence. You'll need to evaluate whether the *but* in question contradicts the preceding statement and see whether *and* is really the word you want. If *and* can be substituted, then *but* is almost certainly the wrong word.

Examples:

He went to work this morning. But he left his briefcase at home.

Between those sentences is an indirect idea, since the two actions are in no way contradictory. What is implied is something like this:

He went to work, intending to give a presentation, but he left his briefcase behind.

Because *and* would have made sense in the original statement, *but* is not the right word.

Correct: He went to work this morning. And he left his briefcase at home.

Nouns

Simply put, a complete sentence must contain a subject [noun] and a verb; and, it should convey a complete thought. The noun names something and contains one or more nouns or pronouns.

What is the sentence's purpose?

Sentences should do one or more of the following:

They make a statement. (I work from home).

They ask a question. (Where do you want to go for dinner?)

They give a command. (Hand me that book.)

They make a request. (Please hand me that book.)

They express a strong feeling. (I cannot believe you did that!)

If a sentence is lacking the subject or a verb, it's known as a fragmented sentence. You'll find sentence fragments in informal writing, but they should not be used in business writing.

Appositive Nouns

An appositive noun is a noun that immediately follows another noun or noun phrase in order to define or further identify it.

Example:

Abraham Lincoln, our sixteenth president, was shot by John Wilkes-Booth.

our sixteenth president is an appositive of the proper noun Abraham Lincoln. It's not essential to the sentence, but it helps us identify Abraham Lincoln.

This leads me to throw in another quick comma tip:

Commas frame an appositive noun (as above) unless the noun or phrase is restrictive. (Restrictive means that it is essential to the meaning of the noun it belongs to.)

Example:
The author John Steinbeck wrote many delightful short stories.

In this case John Steinbeck *restricts* author by precisely identifying which author we're talking about.

Pronouns

Pronouns come in three groups called cases; subjective, objective and possessive. How can you tell whether to use a subjective pronoun or an objective pronoun?

Subjective case - the doer (subject) of the action:
I read the book.

Objective case - the receiver (object) of the action:
Read the book to me.

Possessive case - shows ownership:
My book won the Newbury Award!

To find out if you are using the correct pronoun, either add or delete words to the sentence. Sometimes, you need to turn the sentence around until it sounds right.

What's Wrong With These Sentences?
The chef prepared a special dinner for Tom and I.

Us tired working moms are getting a massage this Tuesday.

Of all the authors in the group, the newest members are Sue and me.

Add Words:

The chef prepared a special dinner for Tom and [for] I.

The chef prepared a special dinner for Tom and [for] me.

Correct: The chef prepared a special dinner for Tom and me.

Delete Words:

Us (delete tired working moms) are getting a massage this Tuesday.

We (delete tired working moms) are getting a massage this Tuesday.

Correct: We tired working moms are getting a massage this Tuesday.

Turn It Around:

Me am newest.

I am newest.

Correct: Of all the authors in the group, the newest members are Sue and I.

Types of Pronouns

A Pronoun is a part of speech used to refer to or replace a noun. There are seven types of pronouns: personal, demonstrative, relative, interrogative, indefinite, reflexive, and reciprocal.

Quickly stated:

A personal pronoun can be a subject *(I, you, he, she, it, we, they)*; an object *(me, you, him, her, it, us, them)*; or a possessive *(my, mine, your, yours, his, her, hers, its, our, ours, their, theirs)*.

A demonstrative pronoun points out something *(this, that, these, those)*.

A relative pronoun introduces a dependent (or subordinate) clause *(that, what, whatever, which, whichever, who, whoever, whom, whomever, whose)*.

An interrogative pronoun is used to ask a question *(what, which, who, whom, whose)*.

An indefinite pronoun refers to a vague or unknown person or thing *(all, another, any, anybody, anyone, anything, both, each, either, every, everybody, everyone, everything, few, many, much, neither, no one, nobody, none, one, other, several, some, somebody, someone, something, such)*.

Grammar

A reflexive pronoun calls attention to itself; it ends with self or selves (*myself, herself, himself, itself*).

Gender-specific Pronouns

Gender-specific pronouns are one of those grammar topics that have writers, editors, and grammar experts split.

Most will strongly object to using *their, they, them* when speaking about one individual, as in: Ask **a friend** if **they** can help.

Like it or not, doing away with gender-specific pronouns is becoming common practice by replacing the generic masculine *he* or *him,* which many now assail as sexist.

And, although you generally don't use a plural pronoun with a singular antecedent, it is becoming more accepted in sentences using words such as *someone* or *anyone*, as in: **Anyone** can join if **they** are a resident.

Many will also agree that *he/she, him/her*, or *s/he* is just plain awkward to read.

So what to do? As a writer, you basically have five (5) choices, and you will have to decide which choice works best. Then be consistent and be prepared to defend your choice.

1) Use they/their

   Examples:

   Someone told me the sky is falling. *They* must be crazy!

   The *employee* asked *their* boss for a longer lunch break.

   The *child* took two new pencils from *their* teacher.

2) Use he/she, he or she, his/her

   Examples:

   Someone told me the sky is falling. *He* or *she* must be crazy!

   The *employee* asked *his/her* boss for a longer lunch break.

   The *child* took two new pencils from *his/her* teacher.

3) Use the generic masculine (he/his)

Examples:

Someone told me the sky is falling. *He* must be crazy!

The *employee* asked *his* boss for a longer lunch break.

The *child* took two new pencils from *his* teacher.

4) Eliminate the pronoun altogether

Examples:

Someone told me the sky is falling. *That person* must be crazy!

The *employee* asked the boss for a longer lunch break.

The *child* took two new pencils from the teacher.

5) Pluralize the antecedent of the pronoun

Examples:

Some people told me the sky is falling. *They* must be crazy!

The *employees* asked *their* boss for a longer lunch break.

The *children* took two new pencils from *their* teacher.

Pronoun-Referent Agreement

Pronoun-referent agreement exists when a sentence's pronoun is in agreement with the noun it is referring to or replacing. Make sure the word a pronoun refers to is clear.

Incorrect:

A manager should not interview a subordinate in her office. (Who's office? The subordinate or the manager?)

Correct:

A manager should not conduct an interview in a subordinate's office.

Prepositions

A preposition is a word or phrase that links an object (a noun or noun equivalent) to another word in the sentence to show the relationship between them.

Some common, simple and compound prepositions include: *as, at, by, for, from, in, of, on, to, with; and, about, after, between, onto, throughout, until, without.* Just to name a few.

Ending a Sentence with a Preposition

There is an antiquated grammar rule still in existence that states one cannot end a sentence with a preposition; however, it is now widely accepted to end a sentence with a preposition. In many cases, ending a sentence with a preposition may sound more natural than a sentence that's cautiously constructed to avoid ending with a preposition. In fact, changing the placement of a preposition can even add creativity to your writing.

Examples of beginning a sentence with a preposition:

Under the sea, sharks unwaveringly stalk their prey.

Between you and me, I'd say this rule is a myth.

During the exam, the students wrote furiously.

Without a ticket, you're sure to miss the event.

Examples of ending a sentence with a preposition:

Don't forget to put on your coat and gloves before you go out.

Tell me what the movie's about.

These are the rules all children should adhere to.

Where are you from?

When NOT to end a sentence with a preposition:

If the ending preposition can be eliminated and the sentence still makes sense, then the ending preposition is unnecessary.

Incorrect: Can you tell me where the library is at?
Incorrect: That's where it's at.
Correct: Can you tell me where the library is?
Correct: That's where it is.

Sentence Type

English has four basic sentence types.

Simple sentences contain one independent clause.

Example:

Donna sells collectibles on eBay.

Compound sentences contain two or more independent clauses.

Example:

Susan finished writing her novel, and now she needs to find an editor.

Complex sentences contain at least one independent clause and one or more dependent clauses.

Example:

After he downloaded the new music to his iPod, Tom updated his new files.

Compound-complex sentences contain two or more independent clauses and at least one dependent clause.

Example:

When Sam was hired, he went through training, yet he couldn't understand the task.

Verbs

It's time to talk about my personal favorite—the verb. I love verbs! They move our sentences. They put people in motion. They show us what is happening in our writing.

There are many verbs to choose from; therefore, your writing will never be boring if you can remember how and when to use verbs correctly. Here are some basics about the verb.

Verbs show action (walk, run, write) or a state of being *(be, feel, smell, seem)*.

Verbs have several characteristics: form, tense, person, number, voice, and mood.

Some verbs can stand alone in a sentence; other verbs are "helping verbs." Helping verbs are forms of the words *do, be,* and *can/may.* They combine with other verbs to form a complete verb phrase *(was sleeping)*.

Still other verbs are called "linking verbs." Linking verbs link the subject of a sentence to a description that follows. Linking verbs include forms of the verb *be* and the verbs *seem, appear, become, grow, remain, stay, prove, feel, look, smell, sound, and taste.*

Verb Forms

Verbs have four primary forms:

Present Form

I work in the Accounting Department.

Past Form [The past form is created by using the present form and adding *d* or *ed.*]

Last year, I worked in the Accounting Department.

Past Participle Form [The past participle form is created by using the past form and adding a helping verb.]

I had worked in the Accounting Department until my recent promotion.

Present Participle Form [The present participle form is created by adding *ing* to the present form and adding a helping verb.]

I will be working in the Finance Department next year.

Verb Person

Verbs are characterized by person (1st, 2nd, or 3rd) and number (singular or plural). They are also characterized by voice and mood.

Make sure the subject of the sentence and the verb agree in person and in number.

Examples:

1st Person - (Singular) I work - (Plural) we work

2nd Person - (Singular) you work - (Plural) you work

3rd Person - (Singular) he, she, it, one, works - (Plural) they work

NOTE: Only the singular 3rd person has an [s] or [es] ending.

Verb Voice

Is your voice active or passive?

If the performer of the action is the subject of the sentence, the verb is in active voice. If the performer of the action is not named or is not the subject of the sentence, the verb is in passive voice.

Because verbs move our sentences and put people in motion, they show us what is happening in our stories. You can see from these examples that the passive voice is less dynamic because it ignores or downplays the doer of the action.

Examples:

Passive Voice:

The meeting was conducted by Susan.

The coat was worn by the man.

A ball was hit and a run was scored.

The car was driven by Tom.

The children were separated into two groups.

The cat was followed by the dog.

The sun will be setting in the west.

Active Voice:

Susan conducted the meeting in the president's absence.

The man wore the coat to ward off the winter wind.

Slugger slammed the ball over the outfield fence scoring the winning run.

Tom drove the car into the lake.

We separated the children into two groups to keep them from fighting.

The Pit Bull chased the frenzied cat up the old oak tree.

The orange glow of daylight threw a veiled shadow over the western mountain range giving way to twilight.

Verb Mood

Moods are changes in the verb to show the speaker's or writer's attitude. English has three moods: the indicative mood (states a fact or opinion or asks a question), the imperative mood (gives a command, request, or warning), and the subjunctive mood (indicates something that is not a fact — a wish, desire, plan, or thought).

Indicative Mood (active voice):
The writer holds the pen.

Indicative Mood (passive voice):
The pen is held by the writer.

Imperative Mood:
Hold the pen.

Subjunctive Mood:
If the pen were held.

NOTE: Keep the mood consistent within a sentence or among related sentences.

Correct: The bank approved the loan. The client signed the papers.

Incorrect: The bank approved the loan. The papers were signed by the client.

Verb Tenses

Tense shows us when an act, state, or condition occurs or occurred. Tenses are divided by time: present, past, and future. Most of the time these present verb forms are easily changed (conjugated) to their past and future tenses (see Verb Forms pg. 53). When they are not, they are considered irregular verbs. Here is a list of several irregular verbs and their sometimes troubling past tenses:

Bring becomes brought (brang and brung are not words)

Drag becomes dragged (drug is often used, but is not correct)

Dive becomes dived or dove

Drive becomes drove or driven (drived is not a word)

Get becomes got or gotten

Hang (to hang a picture or to dangle) becomes hung

Hang (like a horse thief) becomes hanged

Shine (to polish, as in to shine silver) becomes shined

Shine (like the sun, to give off light) becomes shone

Swim becomes swam or swum

Wake becomes woke, waked or woken

Subject-Verb Agreement

It's important to make sure the subject of the sentence and the verb agree in number and in person. A singular subject needs a singular verb, and a plural subject needs a plural verb.

Examples:

The speaker, [singular subject] along with several authors, likes [singular verb] the book's topic.

The speaker along with several authors [plural subject] like [plural verb] the book's topic.

When you have compound subjects joined by and you need a plural verb, unless and separates terms that refer to a single person or is preceded by each, every, or many.

Examples:

My daughter and her friend were here all weekend.

My sister and best friend (same person) is taking me to Jamaica.

Each child and parent is required to be present.

When compound subjects are joined by or or nor they require either a singular or a plural verb, depending on the noun closest to the verb. If one noun is singular and one is plural, put the plural noun last and make the verb plural.

Examples:

My husband or my neighbor is planning the surprise party. (singular subject and verb)

My sons and daughters are planning the surprise party. (plural subject and verb)

My husband or my neighbors are planning the surprise party. (plural subject last)

WORD CHOICE

Word Choice

WORD CHOICE

A and An

Do you get confused about which article to use (*a* or *an*) before words? Here's an easy tip to help you remember.

The choice to use *a* or *an* all comes down to the sound of the word it precedes.

The *a* comes before words with a consonant sound, including *y*, *h*, and *w*, no matter how the word is spelled.

Examples:

a yo-yo

a university

a eulogy

a 100-dollar bill

a hotel suite

The *an* comes before words with a vowel sound, even it that sound is made by a consonant.

Examples:

an oasis

an hour ago (silent h)

an M&M

an X-files episode

an SAT exam

A and This

This is an overused word. It implies something right here, close at hand. Don't use *this* when the word *a* is better.

Examples:

Incorrect: I bought *this* great new dress that I want to show you.

Correct: I bought *a* great new dress that I want to show you.

Incorrect: There's *this* hot new cell phone on the market that I'm dying to buy.

Correct: There's *a* hot new cell phone on the market that I'm dying to buy.

Correct: Look at *this* mess you made!

Correct: Look at *this* splinter in my finger.

Aggravate and Irritate

Irritate means to exasperate, provoke or inflame; aggravate means to make worse or more troublesome.

Example:

A mosquito bite irritates the skin and makes it itch. Scratching the bite aggravates the itch.

The word aggravate is widely used to mean "to irritate," as in "The waiter's surliness aggravated me to no end." But many still insist that the word should be used only to mean "to make worse," in referring to a situation or condition.

Examples:

The plight of the small farmer has been aggravated by the drought.

Susan's bad back was aggravated by her refusal to get sufficient rest.

Aloud vs. Out Loud

Are you reading *aloud* or *out loud?* Are you speaking *out loud* or *aloud?*

This is one of those word usage rules that fall under the semantics rule; they really mean the same thing. Out loud is basically the colloquial equivalent of aloud.

Aloud and **out loud** are both adverbs that mean "in a loud tone; with the voice; orally."

Some grammarians might say to use *aloud* in all but the most casual of settings. I like to use *aloud* when talking about **reading** something, like a passage; and use *out loud* for **speaking**, like a verbal thought spoken.

Examples:

She stood with confidence and read the paragraph *aloud.*

He mumbled his disappointment *out loud,* to no one in particular.

All right vs. Alright

One of the great usage debates of recent times is the spelling of *all right* vs. *alright.*

Usage writers, copy editors, and schoolteachers will argue that *alright* is incorrect despite the ever-increasing frequency of using this form. Yet, others will argue that *alright* is common and acceptable in nonformal contexts.

In common usage, *all right* is a synonym for okay or satisfactory.

Example:

Are you all right?

However, it can also mean "all correct."

Example:

My answers on the test were all right.

In some circles, alright has become an accepted usage interchangeable with most uses of all right, particularly in informal dialogue.

Example:

Rob, do you want to come to the party with me?

Alright.

Generally, most editors and teachers don't think *alright* is *all right.* If you're in doubt, it's best to stick with the more widely accepted two-word *all right,* especially in formal academic or professional writing.

Amid/Among/Between

When should we use amid/among/between?

Use *between* when referring to two individuals or items.

Example:

There was a heated argument between John and Susan at the meeting.

Use *among* when referring to three or more individuals.

Example:

Susan started behaving, among the other members, like a woman possessed.

Use *amid* when the reference is to a quantity of something you don't think of as individual.

Example:

As John stalked off, Susan lost sight of him amid the many chairs.

NOTE: Don't use amidst—it's not correct. And amongst is considered archaic.

Anymore and Everyday

Are you ever confused about when to use *anymore* vs. *any more?* Or *everyday* vs. *every day?*

The word *anymore* is an adverb and means "any longer" or "at the present."

Examples:

Chuck is not the president of the homeowners' association anymore.

Dorothy said to Toto, "We aren't in Kansas anymore."

The two-word phrase *any more* on the other hand, functions as an adjective and therefore modifies (or describes) a noun.

Examples:

Tom does not have any more vacation time left this year.

Susan cannot take any more phone calls right now.

Everyday is an adjective and means encountered or used routinely or typically.

Examples:

The silverware was no longer put to everyday use so was stored as an heirloom.

Walking two miles was an everyday activity for Susan and her dogs.

The two-word phrase *every day* functions as an adverb and describes when an action occurs.

Examples:

The local grocery store advertised it offers substantial savings every day.

Don is late for work nearly every day.

Awhile vs. A While

Will you be staying awhile or staying for a while? Is it one word or two?

Awhile is an adverb that means *for a short time.* When used as such, it should not be proceeded by a preposition, such as *for.*

The two-word form *a while,* is a noun that means *an indefinite period of time* and may be preceded by a preposition.

Examples as an adverb:

You can stay awhile.

Sit down and rest awhile.

That took awhile to learn.

Examples as a noun:

Feel free to stay for a while longer.

Sit down and rest for a while.

That took quite a while to learn.

So, remember, if your sentence calls for a preposition (as, at, by, for, from, in, like, of, on, to, with; just to name a few) then you'll use the two-word noun form.

Blond vs. Blonde

Although both of these words basically have the same meaning, they are different.

blond is mostly used to describe a color (i.e., fair skin or hair or a light-colored wood), and when used as an adjective may be used to describe both sexes.

blonde on the other hand, when used as a noun, is only to describe the female gender.

Eager vs. Anxious

Eager (like excited) primarily suggests a strong interest or desire.

Examples:

I'm eager to go on vacation; it's going to be so much fun.

I'm eager to see the new Spider-Man movie.

Anxious (like anxiety) applies to interest or desire tinged by concern or fear.

Examples:

I'm anxious about our vacation; I hope it's going to be fun.

I'm anxious about taking the SAT.

Ensure vs. Insure

The easiest way to remember the difference between these two is this:

Ensure is to make certain; we ensure your satisfaction, your guarantee, your happiness.

Insure is short for insurance; we insure our property, our car, our home.

Further and Farther

I can never tell if I'm going further or farther. If you, too, have trouble deciding which is correct, hopefully the following definitions will be of help. Use *farther* when referring to physical distance. Use *further* to refer to abstract ideas or to indicate a greater extent or degree and also for time.

Examples:

Susan lives farther from work than I do.

The 10K was a lot farther than I thought.

I want to check into this further. (meaning longer or more in depth)

This working relationship can go no further. (meaning no longer)

In Mexico, the dollar goes further. (meaning more money)

The further back we go, the more indefinite is our family history. (referencing time)

I.E. vs. E.G.

Many people think these two words are interchangeable, but they are not.

i.e. means *that is, in other words,* or more commonly, *namely.* The Latin term is *id est.*

e.g. means for example. The Latin term is *exempli gratia.*

The easiest way to remember this is to use the rule of association: *i.e.* means <u>in</u> other words, and that <u>is</u>; both have the letter "i."

And, *e.g.* means for <u>example</u>; both have an "e."

It should, also, be noted that **i.e.** and **e.g.** are not italicized, and they are best used in lists, parenthetical statements, and citations rather than in text.

Examples:

The U.S. has many states that begin with the letter A (i.e., Alabama, Alaska, Arizona).

French Fries go well with dipping sauce (e.g, ketchup, ranch dressing).

When it comes to using these terms in text, it's more acceptable to write out the meaning instead of using the abbreviation.

Examples:

The U.S. has many states that begin with the letter A, namely (or in other words, that is), Alabama, Alaska, Arizona.

French Fries go well with a dipping sauce, for example, ketchup, ranch dressing.

A word about punctuation. Because these are abbreviations, always use a period after each letter (but no spaces) and it's recommended by most style manuals to use a comma following **i.e.** and **e.g.** just as you would if you were spelling them out.

In/On Behalf Of

Are you doing something *in* behalf of or *on* behalf of someone else? *In* behalf of means "for the benefit of," or "in the interest of." *On* behalf of means "in place of," or "as the agent of."

Example:

Susan presented the check on behalf of the Writer's Club, to be used in behalf of those that could not attend.

In To vs. Into

Yes, there is a difference! Just because *in* and *to* happen to land next to each other often in writing, don't be too quick to combine them as one word.

Into is for entering something (like a room or a profession), for changing the form of something (like an ugly duckling), or for making contact (with a friend or a wall).

Example:

He walked into the boss's office and bumped into the door on his way in.

Otherwise, use in to.

If you can drop the *in* without losing the meaning, then you are correct in using *in to*.

Example:

Bring the clients [in] to the waiting room and we'll go [in] to the board room for the meeting.

Lay vs. Lie

Remember: Lay is an active verb. Lay means "to place." Lie is a "still" or passive verb. Lie means "to recline."

Examples of Lay:

Lay the book on the desk.

Lay your cares aside.

The hen lays an egg.

See, it's active. The verb is doing something.

Examples of Lie:

She lies quietly.

Lie down on the bed and take a nap.

Roll over and lie on your side.

The verb is being very "still" here. No action.

The only time lie becomes lay is in the past tense form:

lay, laid, laying

lie, lay, lain, lying

Examples:

Lay the books on the desk.

Yesterday, I laid the books on the desk.

Laying the books on the desk caused a smudge mark.

Today I lie in bed.

Yesterday, I lay in bed for hours.

I could have lain there all day.

Lying in bed all day would be very boring.

Less vs. Fewer

There are several rules for the *less* vs. *fewer* rule. Although these two words both mean the opposite of *more*, they are used differently.

Simply put, *less* applies to singular nouns and *fewer* applies to plural nouns.

Let's put this is terms of items at the grocery store checkout lane. The sign at the store reads: 15 Items or Less. Grammatically, this is incorrect, because "items" is plural; therefore, fewer would be used.

To correct this sign, it should read: 1 Item or Less, but this would be ridiculous since less than one would be zero and therefore no need for a sign at all.

Examples:

Less fattening [singular], but fewer calories [plural]

Less of a burden [singular], but fewer burdens [plural]

Less water [singular], but fewer glasses [plural] of water

Less furniture [singular], but fewer chairs [plural]

But wait . . .

What about time, money, miles and periods of time? Are these singular or plural nouns? Do we use less or fewer?

Typically, time, money, miles, and periods of time use *less* mainly because, although these items appear to be plural, they are considered individual [singular] units of measures.

Like vs. As or As If

Like is probably the least-understood preposition. It's used to compare one thing to another. It means *similar to* or *for example*.

Examples:

This flower looks *like* a daisy.

This tastes more *like* lemonade than iced tea.

You look *like* your father.

I'm good at water sports *like* skiing and sailing.

As and *as if* are conjunctions used before clauses. (Remember: a clause has a subject and a verb.)

Examples:

He worked hard *as* he knew he should.

You look *as if* you've seen a ghost.

May vs. Might

It's tricky not to get these two words confused. May comes from the word maybe, and that's a good indicator for when it's used. May indicates the probability that something's happening or going to happen. Might is the weaker form of may; something that might happen doesn't mean it will. Try substituting the word maybe as your guide if you're not sure.

Examples:

I might get an award at the reception tonight. (It's a possibility, but not probable.) Can you substitute maybe here? No! I maybe get an award at the reception tonight.

Having the operation may have saved her life. (It's probable because she's still alive.) Can you substitute maybe here? Yes! Although, it is not exactly grammatically correct. Having the operation maybe saved her life.

Even though you are tempted to use might in that sentence, don't, it makes for a weaker sentence. The operation might have saved her life. (Well, did it or didn't it?)

Me, Myself, or I

I don't know where or how the use of using *myself* in a sentence, in place of *I* or *me* began, but grammarians will agree that we wish it would stop. Perhaps saying *I* or *me* seemed a bit egotistical, so people began to replace these pronouns with the more polite sounding *myself.*

If you find that you get confused on when to use me, I, or myself, here is a trick to remember this rule: Whenever you think you should use *myself* in a sentence, remember, you'll be **self**-ish if you do, and you will know that *I* or *me* is probably the better choice.

Examples:

Incorrect: Tom and *myself* were invited to the party.

Correct: Tom and *I* were invited to the party.

Tip: If you remove Tom from the sentence, you would simply state, "I was invited to the party," not "Myself was invited to the party."

Incorrect: Speaking at the seminar helped sell hundreds of books for Susan and myself.

Correct: Speaking at the seminar helped sell hundreds of books for Susan and me.

Tip: Once again, if you remove Susan from the sentence, you would state, "... the seminar helped sell hundreds of books for me," not, "...for myself."

When is it okay to be **self**-ish? When the sentence refers to the subject.

Examples:

I'm going to treat *myself* to a massage.

I've been teaching *myself* to play the piano.

When used to emphasize.

Examples:

I made those cookies *myself.*

I carried those heavy boxes by *myself.*

This rule also works with the other *self* pronouns (called reflexive pronouns), herself, himself, itself, yourself, ourselves, themselves.

Nauseated vs. Nauseous

What's the difference between nauseated and nauseous?

It's the difference between being sick and sickening. Try to remember: you are made sick (nauseated) by something sickening (nauseous).

You'll hear a lot of people say, "I'm nauseous," but I wouldn't admit it, because that would mean you are sickening. You are more likely to be nauseated by that nauseous odor.

So next time you are feeling nauseated, lie down until the feeling goes away!

Of vs. With

Are we bored *of* or bored *with*? Is it *could of been* or *could have been*? *Must of* or *must have*?

This is easy to remember. *Could of* does not exist. Neither does *should of, will of, must of* or *would of.*

The correct way is to use the word *have.* Write *could have, should have, will have, must have* or *would have.* If you want to emphasize the pronunciation, write it as a verb contraction: could've, should've, must've or would've.

Only

"Only the lonely" is the phrase to remember when trying to figure out where this word belongs. Only means alone, solely, or no other. In order to be grammatically correct, put only right before the word or phrase you want to emphasis.

Examples:

Incorrect: I'm only going to say this once.

Correct: I'm going to say this only once.

Incorrect: I only have three dollars.

Correct: I have only three dollars.

And don't use only in place of *except* or *but.*

Examples:

Incorrect: I would have gone on the cruise only I was broke.

Correct: I would have gone on the cruise except I was broke.

Correct: I would have gone on the cruise but I was broke.

Past vs. Passed

Are we walking past your house, or passed your house? Did the car speed passed or speed past the stop sign?

Many writers get these two words mixed up. And it's no wonder.

Past can be used as an adjective, noun or adverb and typically relates to location and describes something in time, and sometimes in space.

Passed is typically a verb, but there are a few occasions when it can be used as a noun or an adjective. Passed is the past tense, and the past participle, of the verb **to pass**. To pass means to proceed, move forward, depart; to cause to do something. This can refer to movement forwards in time, in space, or in life.

Passed can also be an intransitive verb (one which doesn't require an object) or a transitive verb (one which requires both a subject and one or more objects).

So when do *past* and *passed* get confused and how can we keep them straight? Let's examine the following examples.

Incorrect: The climbers past a stream on their way to the top of Mt. Evans.

Correct: The climbers passed a stream on their way to the top of Mt. Evans.

In this sentence *passed* is the past participle of the verb *to pass*.

One trick to help you remember is to rewrite the sentence in the present tense, as though you're describing something that is happening now.

The climbers pass a stream on their way to the top of Mt. Evans.

The climbers are passing a stream on their way to the top of Mt. Evans.

However, if you wrote:

The climbers walked past a stream on their way to the top of Mt. Evans.

You'd be correct, because in this sentence the verb is *walked*; therefore, *past* is acting as an adverb.

Examples of Past:

Past as an adjective meaning elapsed, gone by in time, done with, over:

The days for celebrating are now past.

All past presidents of the United States were male.

Past as a noun meaning time that has gone by, before the present.

In the past, our company's standards were higher.

We cannot continue to live in the past.

Past as a preposition can mean beyond in time; after; as in stating the time of day.

We'll meet you at half past seven.

It can also be used for location, beyond in place, further on than, at or on the further side of, to a point beyond:

My house is the one just past the first stop sign on the left.

Past as an adverb as to pass or go by.

The car sped past the stop sign.

Examples of Passed:

Passed as an *intransitive* verb:

The days [subject] passed quickly. [no object]

Passed as a *transitive* verb:

I [subject] passed my driving test. [object]

He [subject] passed the football [object] like a pro.

People vs. Persons

Do you know which of these sentences is correct?

Susan was one of the nicest persons I've ever met.
Or
Susan was one of the nicest people I've ever met?

This is tricky because the meaning of both words is nearly identical. Both words refer to groups of humans; however, traditionally, people describes a general group while persons portrays a smaller, more specific group.

Examples:

More than 30,000 *people* attended the ball game. (The attendees are considered a large general group.)

The nine *persons* in the front row wore team jerseys. (Those wearing team jerseys are specific; therefore, *persons* is the better choice.)

BUT . . .
The use of the word persons isn't too popular anymore, and reference guides now recommend using persons if it's in a direct quote or part of a title (i.e., Bureau of Missing Persons).

SO . . .

The correct choice in the sentence above would be:

Susan is one of the nicest people I've ever met.

Phew and Whew

Phew and Whew are interjections [an exclamation denoting strong feelings]. One could easily replace the other depending on your sentence. These two interjections are usually found at the beginning of a sentence.

Phew is used to express relief, fatigue, surprise, or disgust.

Example:

Phew! I can't believe I climbed to the top of the Empire State Building.

Whew is used to express strong emotions such as relief or amazement.

Example:

Whew! Do you see how many stairs there are to climb to the top of the Empire State Building?

P.S.

The earliest known use of P.S. goes back to 1523, when handwritten letters were the only mode of communication. The letter writer added the addendum in order to give the information left out of the main body of text, to prevent having to rewrite the entire letter. In those days, an expensive and time consuming task!

In the modern world of computerized letters and e-mail, P.S. is still used to highlight something not contained in the original letter.

So, is it written: P.S. and then P.P.S. or P.S.S.? And what exactly does P.S. stand for?

P.S. stands for the Latin word, *postscriptum* (postscript) which means adding an addendum to the main body of text.

P.P.S. would therefore represent post-postscript.

P.S.S. would be an error or confusion for P.P.S., unless it is used for an acronym, but should not be used to add a note to the end of a letter.

The use of P.P.S. is to give extra emphasis to something else not included in the body of the original text or the first postscript.

It is also readily used today as a marketing ploy, to get an important item noticed by the readers who have a tendency to skim content, rather than read every word.

Racked vs. Wracked

Let's face it. There are just some words, even though we know how to spell them, we're just not sure if we are using them correctly.

Are you racked with guilt, or wracked? Is tax time nerve-racking, or nerve-wracking? Are you on the brink of rack and ruin, or wrack and ruin?

Most of the time, you are racked (tortured, strained, stretched, punished) like in the medieval torture rack. If you're wracked, you're destroyed—you're washed up (the words wrack and wreck are related).

Examples:
You are racked with guilt.

You've had a nerve-racking experience.

But, you are a nervous wreck.

You're facing wrack and ruin.

Stationery vs. Stationary

The stationery (paper) stays stationary (fixed or still) on the table. Here's the trick: Both stationery and paper contain "er."

Than vs. Then

Than and **then** are commonly confused when writing. *Than* is used as a comparison and is commonly a conjunction, but can also be used as a preposition. *Then* is used as a time expression and can be a noun, adverb, or adjective depending on the sentence structure.

Examples using than:
She is a better athlete *than* I.

I would rather ride *than* walk.

We disliked the movie more *than* them.

She's worked here longer *than* I have.

His writing is very different *than* mine.

Examples using then:

I was younger *then*.

I watched the late night news and *then* went to bed.

He lost the election, but *then* we never expected him to win.

If you're always late, *then* you better go now.

Until *then*, let's stay here.

It'll take all his strength and *then* some.

Thankful and Thankfully

Thankful [adjective] is an expressions of thanks. Of being grateful.

In the mid-1960s, the word *thankfully* [adverb] came into use in the sense "thank goodness; I am (or we are) thankful that...." Although this use of *thankfully* is now fairly common, it doesn't represent the best usage.

Here are some examples where thankfully could (and should) be replaced with a more acceptable term.

Examples:

I can assure you that my party will have food, dancing, and *thankfully* [read thank goodness], lots of beer.

At the age of two, my daughter spoke in incomprehensible phrases, but *thankfully* [read fortunately], by three, she had graduated to complete sentences.

Thankfully [read luckily], I was able to stop the car before the motorcyclist darted in front of me.

That

There are two kinds of editors. One sticks in *that* wherever it will fit. The other takes it out. Some believe that if *that* can logically follow a verb, it should be there. Others believe that if *that* can logically be omitted, it should be taken out.

So what's the rule? It's purely a matter of taste. If the sentence sounds better with *that* then use it. If it sounds fine without it, then don't.

Here are some cases where adding *that* can save your reader confusion:

When a time element comes after the verb:
Bob said on Friday he would confess.

This could mean either: Bob said that on Friday he would confess, or Bob said on Friday that he would confess. Add *that* to make your sentence clear.

When the point of the sentence comes late:
Frank found the old violin hidden in a trunk in his attic wasn't a real Stradivarius.

Better: Frank found *that* the old violin hidden in a trunk in his attic wasn't a real Stradivarius. Otherwise, we have to read to the end of the sentence to learn that Frank finding the violin isn't the point.

When there are two more verbs after the main one:
Susan thinks the idea stinks and Bob does too.

What exactly is Susan thinking? It could mean Susan thinks that the idea stinks, and that Bob does too. Adding *that* (and a well-placed comma) can make clear who's thinking what.

That vs. Who

Which is correct: "The girl that got the promotion" or "The girl who got the promotion?"

Do they both sound right? That's because they both are right.

A *person* can be either a *that* or a *who*. A *thing*, on the other hand, is always a *that*.

But what about animals? They aren't people, but they aren't quite things. Are animals a that or a who?

Examples:
If the animal is anonymous (as in, we don't know its name), it is a *that*:
There's the dog that gets into my garbage every week.

If the animal has a name, he or she is a *who*:

Ginger is the dog who gets into my garbage every week.

Toe the Line vs. Tow the Line

We may think of towing (or pulling) a boat or cord, when we hear the idiom "towing the line," but this phrase is actually called, "toeing the line" and means to touch a mark or line with the toe or hands in readiness for the start of a race or competition.

Toeing the line used in today's English means to conform to the rules or a standard. Just like the runner who "toes the line" is one who does not allow his foot to stray over the line. Therefore, he is said to not drift beyond a rigidly defined boundary.

Examples:

Movies these days don't always *toe the line* of decency.

The candidate is expected to *toe the line* while campaigning.

It was high time for him to *toe the line*.

Toward vs. Towards

Both of these words are correct and interchangeable. You can use either one because they mean the same thing, but many reference manuals state that attaching the [s] is used mostly in British English and without the [s] is preferred in American English.

Another tidbit about the word toward is its pronunciation. Toward is pronounced /tord (rhymes with board) - not /tword or /tward.

Toward, like backward, implies movement.

Examples:

The horses knew they were headed toward home.

He likes to sit with his back toward the wall.

It began to rain toward morning.

Mom didn't like her teenager's attitude toward her father.

He threw in five dollars toward the bill.

Their efforts toward peace were successful.

Well/Good and Bad/Badly

Let's meet Well/Good and their neighbors Bad/Badly. If you can keep this rule straight, you've got this problem licked!

Good and bad are adjectives (they modify a noun). When a condition or a passive state is being described, use the adjectives good or bad.

Examples:

After the two-day conference, Sam [noun] looked bad.

Susan [noun], on the other hand, looked good.

I [noun] feel bad.

Susan [noun] feels good.

When it's an activity being described, use the adverb (modifies a verb) badly or well.

Examples:

Sam ran [verb] the race badly.

Sam did [verb] well on his presentation.

Susan sang [verb] well at the opening ceremonies.

She played [verb] well too.

Who vs. Whom

Grammarians now say that whom is on its way out and that who should be able to do the job of both. For conversations and informal writing, who is becoming more acceptable. For formal written documents, it's still best to use whom.

But if you don't know who is whom and whom is who, let me show you:

The most important thing to remember when it comes to whom vs. who is:

Who does something (it's a subject, like he), and

Whom has something done to it (it's an object like him).

So ask yourself who is doing what to whom and try mentally substituting he or him where who or whom should go. If him fits, you want *whom* (they both end in "m"). If **he** fits, you want *who* (both end in a vowel).

Who's vs. Whose

The confusion on whether to use *who's* vs. *whose* comes from thinking that the apostrophe (which on 99% of English words indicates possession), but with this pronoun, it simply indicates a contraction of who is or who has.

When you get confused on whether to use who's vs. whose, try to remember that if you can insert *is* or less commonly, *has*, after the word *who*, then use the contraction. If not, use *whose*, which, by the way is the possessive form of *who*.

Examples:

Who's (who is) driving that car?

Who's (who is) the leader of the band?

Who's (who is) at the top of the best seller list?

There goes the man who's (who has) done it all.

Whose car is this?

Whose band is playing tonight?

Whose best seller is at the top of the list?

Whose side are you on?

Whose vs. Of Which

The relative *who* and *which* can both take *whose* as a possessive form (*whose* substitutes for *of which*).
Some writers object to using *whose* as a replacement for *of which* especially when the subject is not human. I use the possessive *whose* because it's smoother; less awkward sounding.

Compare:

The company whose stock rose faster gained the most for its employees. The company, the stock of which rose faster, gained the most for its employees.

A book, the conclusion of which is unforgettable, keeps the reader wanting more.

A book *whose* conclusion is unforgettable keeps the reader wanting more.

Yay, Yeah and Yea

Many people get confused by the terms Yay, Yeah, and Yea.

The word *yea* is an archaic formal way of saying yes that was used mainly in voting. It's the opposite of, and rhymes with, *nay*.

Example:

All in favor of ordering pizza, say yea.

All opposed say, nay.

When writing the common casual version of yes the correct spelling is *yeah* (sounds like yeh).

Examples:

Yeah, I've heard of that terminology before.

Yeah! Rock and Roll lives forever!

The word *yay* also rhymes with nay but is the opposite of *boo* (as in the negative, not the scary).

Examples:

When the piping hot pizza arrived, we all yelled "yay!"

Yay! The concert starts in five minutes!

STYLE & USAGE

Style & Usage

Are You Asking "Yourself?"

We often see people write:

While rummaging through the car, I *asked myself,* Now where did I put those keys? Or, While rummaging through the car, I *thought to myself,* Now where did I put those keys?

In both sentences the statements asked *myself* and *thought to myself* are redundant.

It's evident that I am talking to no one but myself, so why repeat and write the word *myself?*

It all comes down to a matter of personal writing style, but make sure your dialogue is clear to your reader.

Example:

You are in a computer store with your friend Bill, trying to decide between two competing printers. Besides Bill, a salesperson is there with you.

"This one is less expensive," I said.

"But the print quality is very poor," remarked Bill.

"Yes, but with this model, you can glean all the benefits of the 7100 without compromising performance," said the salesperson.

"That model is $300.00 more! Is he only thinking about his commission?" I *asked.*

By only writing, *I asked,* am I asking Bill, the salesperson, myself, or just a thought spoken out loud to no one in particular?

In this dialogue example it would be important to add the word *myself,* otherwise leave it out.

Clichés

What do these statements have in common?

Blind as a bat, cool as a cucumber, and slept like a baby—they are all clichés; an overused expression that a million writers have used before you and a million more will use after you.

The English language has enough words for writers to be creative. So, why use the same-old, same-old? Let's try to be creative!

Here are a few other worn-out clichés to keep out of your writing:

To beat the band

In a jiffy

Sick as a dog

As plain as the nose on my face

Easy as pie

Skinny as a rail

Raining cats and dogs

Strong as an ox

Thick as thieves

Eat your heart out

Down in the dumps

Tight as a drum

Hard as nails

Fresh as a daisy

Diction

Selecting the correct words

Although important in all communication, choosing the correct words are especially important in writing, where ideas and attitudes are expressed without the help of facial expressions, tone of voice, or gestures. You can enhance the power of your writing by following these guidelines:

Use the correct word

Beware of confusing words that sound alike and have related or similar meanings (*imply/infer; convex/concave; disinterested/uninterested; emigrate/immigrate*). For example, to *imply* means to suggest but not express something. ("His silence *implied* anger.") To *infer* means to deduce or arrive at a conclusion from facts on hand. ("We *inferred* from his tone of voice that he was angry.")

Use descriptive words

Whenever possible, use a descriptive word over a vague word. Words such as *thing* and *stuff* and weak verbs such as *walk, act, move* can often be replaced by words that convey a more precise meaning.

Example:

Vague: My brother drove up in a rundown car.

Better: My brother sputtered to a stop in his old, dilapidated convertible.

Use appropriate words

Words that are right in one situation may be wrong in another (i.e., female siblings, is an acceptable expression by itself), but it would be awkward to use as follows:

Example:

Awkward: Jan, Sylvia, and I are best friends as well as female siblings.

Better: Jan, Sylvia, and I are best friends as well as sisters.

Figures of Speech

A figure of speech is a mode of expression in which words are taken out of their literal meaning to create a more vivid or dramatic picture for your reader or listener. Did you know there are over 20 different Figures of Speech? Here are some of my favorites for improving your writing or storytelling. Learn these important figures of speech and watch your writing soar!

Alliterations

Matching or repetition of consonants or repeating of the same letter (or sound) at the beginning of words. Alliterations are used extensively in poetry writing.

Examples:

Papa's potatoes and poultry were a big hit at the potluck.

Dewdrops danced on the Day Lilies' tongue.

Don't Delay!

Colloquialism

Colloquialisms are informal expressions (also thought of as slang) that should never be used in formal speech or writing, but play a role in how we communicate. You'll find many colloquialisms used in everyday speech.

Examples:

Gonna and wanna

What's his beef?

There ain't nothin' to it

There's more than one way to skin a cat

I grew up in a one-horse town

Heteronyms

Heteronyms are words that are spelled the same but differ in meaning *and* pronunciation.

Examples:

attribute - (at-TRIB-ute) to ascribe; (AT-trib-ute) characteristic

bowed - (rhymes with "how'd") inclined the head in greeting; (rhymes with "towed") bent

close - (CLOZE) to shut; (CLOHSS) nearby

conduct - (CON-duct) behavior; (con-DUCT) to direct or manage

digest - (DIE-jest) collection of published material; (die-JEST) absorb nutrients

dove - (rhymes with "love") a bird; (rhymes with "hove") jumped off

entrance - (EN-trance) entry way; (en-TRANCE) to captivate

house - (HOWSS) building that serves as living quarters; (HOWZ) to provide with living quarters

incense - (IN-cense) substance that produces a pleasant aroma when burned; (in-CENSE) to anger

lead - (LEED) to guide; (LED) a metallic element

minute - (MIN-it) sixty seconds; (my-NOOT) tiny

number - (NUM-ber) a discrete value or quantity; (NUM-mer) more numb

object - (OB-ject) thing; (ob-JECT) to protest

perfect - (PER-fect) flawless; (per-FECT) to make flawless

refuse - (REF-yoos) garbage; (ref-YOOZ) to deny

separate - (SEP-ar-ATE) to set apart; (SEP-ret) not joined together

tear - (TARE) to rip; (TEER) a drop of the clear liquid emitted by the eye

wound - (WOOND) to injure; (WOWND) coiled up

Homonyms

Homonyms are words that are spelled and pronounced the same but differ in meaning or derivation.

Examples:

Bank (a place to deposit money), and **bank** (a river's edge)

Fair (county fair), fair (reasonable), **fair** (appearance as in fair skinned)

Homophones

Homophones are words that are pronounced the same but differ in meaning, origin, and sometimes spelling.

Examples:

Cite (to quote as an authority or example), **sight** (to see), site (location or place)

Sea (body of water), and **see** (vision)

Bow (tie or package ornament), and **bough** (branch of a tree)

Hyperboles

A hyperbole [pronounced "hy-PER-buh-lee"] is a figure of speech that adds exaggeration to your writing. Hyperboles are often confused with similes and metaphors because they sometimes compare two objects. Hyperbole statements are not literally true, but people use them to sound impressive and to emphasize something, such as feelings, efforts, or reactions.

The tall tales your grandfather told you about catching that 20-pound trout are examples of hyperbole.

Examples of hyperbole:
Her feet were as big as skis.

I nearly died laughing.

I'm so hungry I could eat a horse.

He's as big as a house.

I've heard that joke a thousand times.

Malapropism

Named after Richard Sheridan's character Mrs. Malaprop in *The Rivals,* malapropisms are a comic misuse of language.

Examples:
He had to use a fire distinguisher.

Dad says the monster is just a pigment of my imagination.

My sister has extra-century perception.

What are you incinerating, that I'll fade into Bolivian?

Metaphors

The metaphor is the most common figure of speech. It lets us use one image to conjure up another. You hear metaphors used every day and some we've heard so often they are now considered clichés.

Metaphors are different than similes, although they are often confused because they both show a comparison of two different things. Whereas a simile is *like something* else, a metaphor *is something* else.

Examples of Metaphors:

All the world's a stage

Love is war

Life is a journey

You are my sunshine

Time flies

Examples of Metaphors Used in Writing:

The thick blanket of snow covered the frozen field.

His explosive temper erupted causing his magma of emotion to heat everyone around him.

The young girl was a butterfly flittering from one activity to another.

NOTE: What you don't want to do is mix your metaphors; otherwise, your two competing images will drown each other out and your reader will be thoroughly confused.

Examples of Mixed Metaphors:

Don't count your chickens till the cows come home.

She saw the cloud's silver lining at the end of the tunnel.

He stepped up to the plate and grabbed the bull by the horns.

Don't beat a dead horse, because you can't make him drink.

Oxymoron

One of my favorite figures of speech is the oxymoron. An oxymoron takes two incongruous or contradictory terms and puts them together to express two contrasting qualities in one concept.

We've all heard the famous jumbo shrimp and pretty ugly, but here is a list of some of my all time favorite oxymora (that's plural for oxymoron).

Examples:

mandatory option - how can an option be mandatory?

old news - how can news, which is current, be old?

dull roar - can a roar really be dull?

same difference - if it's different, how can it be the same?

bitter sweet - if it's bitter, how can it be sweet?

half naked - you are either naked or you're not.

random order - can something in order be random?

recorded live - is it live or is it recorded?

alone together - are we alone or are we together?

plastic silverware - is the eating utensil made of plastic or silver?

healthy tan - studies show there is no such thing as a healthy tan?

sight unseen - am I seeing it or not?

open secret - if it's a secret, how can it be open?

living dead - are they zombies?

civil war - since when is war civil?

even odds - which is it, even or odd?

good grief - can grief be good?

Palindrome

A palindrome is a word, phrase, verse, or sentence that reads the same backward or forward.

Examples:

Straw - warts

Do geese see God?

Never odd or even

Pangram

A pangram is a phrase or sentence that uses all 26 letters of the alphabet.

Examples:

The quick brown fox jumps over a lazy dog.

Watch Jeopardy!, Alex Trebek's fun TV quiz game.

Personification

Personification is a figure of speech that gives "human" characteristics (emotion, honesty, volition, etc.) to an animal, object, or idea.

Examples of Personification:
The haughty peacock strutted around his mate.

Fate frowned on her success.

My car was happy to be washed.

Pleonasms

Pleonasms are the opposites (antonyms) of oxymora. A pleonasm consists of two concepts (usually two words) that are redundant.

Examples:
at this point in time (use either: at this point or at this time)

bare naked

boiling hot

cash money

climb up

dark night

empty hole

fall down

free gift

freezing cold

good luck

ISBN number (International Standard Book Number, therefore *number* twice is redundant)

join together

little baby

mutual cooperation

original founder

pair of twins

personal friend

repeat again

serious danger

sudden impulse

tiny speck

top priority

unexpected surprise

unsolved mystery

VIN number (**V**ehicle **I**dentification **N**umber)

Similes

You will usually find the words "as" or "like" when using a simile. The simile is a comparison that show how two things that are not alike in most ways are *similar* in another way.

Examples of Common Similes:

Busy as a beaver

Sly as a fox

Eat like a horse

Examples of Emotion Similes:

Mad as a wet hen

Happy as a lark

Cried like a baby

Examples of Similes Used in Writing:

The snow was as thick as a down blanket.

His temper exploded like a volcano.

She swam the medley as easy as a dolphin.

Slang

What about using slang when writing? It depends on what you are writing and who will read it. Slang is great in its place. Out of place, slang makes you and your writing sound dumb or disrespectful.

Take the following letters for example:

Dear Mr. Smith,
Thank you for your generous offer of two tickets to the Rockies/Yankees base-
ball game, which I accept with gratitude and excitement. I look forward to
watching the Rockies win!
I send my best wishes to you and your family.
Sincerely,
John Johnson

Yo, Dawg!
Thanks, dude! The tickets to the game are awesome! How cool! I am major
pumped to watch the Rocks kick the Yanks to the curb. Come over to my crib
sometime and we'll grab some grub and chill.
Later,
JJ

If you wrote the first letter to your best friend, you would sound like a real nerd. If you wrote the second letter to your boss, you would most likely never get tickets again.

Spoonerism

Spoonerisms are words or phrases in which letters or syllables get swapped.

Examples:

I'm driving in the right lane, for *I'm driving in a light rain.*

Tease my ears, for *Ease my tears*

Wave the sails, for *Save the whales*

Commonly Misspelled Words

Hundreds of words are commonly misspelled in the English language. Since I can't list them all in this book, I'll give my top A-Z picks for the most commonly misspelled words and give you tips to help you remember.

accommodate - This word is long enough to accommodate both a double [c] AND a double [m].

believe - You must believe that [i] really does come before [e] in this word.

collectible - There's no [table] to put your collectibles on.

definite(ly) - There is no [ate] in the [finite] art of dining so definitely don't replace [it] with and [a].

equipment - This word has a level playing field, an extra [t] makes it look awkward [equiptment].

fiery - If you remember the [fire] swallowed the [e] and got stuck in between, you'll never have a problem.

gauge - Gauge rhymes with [age] then plop in a [u].

harass - Unlike accommodate, this word is too small to for a double [r] AND a double [s]. So, one [r] will do.

ignorance - Remember to dance the ignorance dance because this word ends in [ance] not [ence].

judgment - [e] leaves the building when [judge] and [ment] come together.

liaison - Two [i's] and an [s] that sounds like a [z] makes this word the go between.

misspell - Just remember this word is [mis] + [spell].

privilege - Again, two [i's] and two [e's] in that order and no [d] in between.

questionnaire - [Question] + [naire] makes for a double [n] and a silent [e] at the end.

rhyme - If you break this word down and sound it out slowly [rh-y-m] then change the [i sound] to a [y] and add a silent [e], you'll remember this word and be happy as can be.

separate - There's no separatism here; the two [e's] surround the two [a's].

twelfth - If you pronounce this word correctly you'll hear the [f] and remember to always leave it in.

until - There is only one [l] in until. Repeat after me . . . one [l], one [l], one [l]. Say it three times and you'll never forget.

vacuum - My vacuum goes vroom, which has two [o's], so my vacuum must have two [u's] in order to go.

weird - Hmmm, now what's that rule again? [i] before [e] except after [w]?

Commonly Mispronounced Words

Many times if you pronounce a word correctly, it will usually help you with the spelling. Here is my top A-Z picks for the most commonly mispronounced words and tips to help you remember.

It's Not Pronounced: acrossed
It Is Pronounced: across
Remember: We are not going acrossed the street, we are going across the street.

It's Not Pronounced: bobbed wire
It Is Pronounced: barbed wire
Remember: I don't think Bob invented this wire, but I do know it is full of barbs.

It's Not Pronounced: chester drawers
It is Pronounced: chest of drawers
Remember: We're not talking about Chester's underwear, but we are talking about a chest of drawers he can put them in.

It's Not Pronounced: dialate
It Is Pronounced: dilate
Remember: The [i] in this word is so long, there's time to put in another vowel, but don't.

It's Not Pronounced: excetera
It Is Pronounced: et cetera
Remember: Two separate words meaning "and" [et] "the rest" [cetera]. There is no [x] sound.

It's Not Pronounced: foilage
It Is Pronounced: foliage
Remember: The [i] comes after the [l], as in "folio."

It's Not Pronounced: heighth
It Is Pronounced: height
Remember: We're not measuring the heighth and width, but the height and width.

It's Not Pronounced: irregardless
It Is Pronounced: regardless
Remember: "Less" tells us "without" so "ir" is redundant.

It's Not Pronounced: jewlery
It Is Pronounced: jewelry
Remember: We are talking about "jewels" here so "jewel-ry" is correct.

It's Not Pronounced: libary
It Is Pronounced: library
Remember: This is right up there with February; there are two [r]s and they are both pronounced.

It's Not Pronounced: miniture
It Is Pronounced: miniature
Remember: There are three syllables in this word for tiny; don't forget the middle [a].

It's Not Pronounced: nuptual
It Is Pronounced: nuptial
Remember: Although there is a "you" in nuptial, there is no [u] so don't pronounce it.

It's Not Pronounced: often
It Is Pronounced: ofen
Remember: This is one exception where you don't pronounce the word the way it is spelled. The [t] is silent.

It's Not Pronounced: perscription
It Is Pronounced: prescription
Remember: This one is pronounced the way it is spelled, using the suffix [pre].

It's Not Pronounced: realator
It Is Pronounced: realtor
Remember: There is no extra [a] in realtor.

It's Not Pronounced: spittin' image
It Is Pronounced: spit and image
Remember: The very spit of someone is an exact likeness. "The spit and image" or "spit image," emphasizes the exactness.

It's Not Pronounced: triathalon
It Is Pronounced: triathlon
Remember: I know it's hard to think of a [th] right next to an [l] without inserting a vowel, but don't.

It's Not Pronounced: upmost
It Is Pronounced: utmost
Remember: Sure, the word does indicate that efforts are up, but the word is "utmost."

It's Not Pronounced: verbage
It Is Pronounced: verbiage
Remember: Don't lose the [i] when pronouncing this word. It will also help you spell it correctly.

It's Not Pronounced: warsh
It Is Pronounced: wash
Remember: We're not warshing the clothes, we are washing them.

The Compound Re-

Many compounds may be formed with *re-,* which means anew, as in rebuild; or back, as in react; or when used as an intensive, as in refine. It all comes down to readability, structure, and often, pronunciation.

In forming compounds, *re-* is normally joined with its following element without a space or hyphen.

Examples:

reopen

reunify

reposition

refill

If the second element begins with *e,* it is preferable to separate it with a hyphen; however, such compounds may often be found written together and are perfectly acceptable.

Examples:

re-entry or reentry

re-edit or reedit

If a compound resembles a familiar word and is intended in a special sense, the hyphen is necessary to make the distinction.

Examples:

re-creation could be confused for recreation

re-cover could be confused for recover

The hyphen may also be necessary to clarify an unusual word formation or a compound that produces a series of three or more vowels.

Examples:

re-realignment

re-aerify

As always, check your dictionary when you are unsure.

Cutting Out Unnecessary Words

Words communicate what we think, feel and do. The more complex the idea or thought, the more difficult it is to express it precisely. Your choice of words should be based on what will be clear for your reader.

Here's a sample list of some alternative words for common, wordy expressions:

Instead of:	Use:
with regard to	about
by means of	by
in the event that	if
until such time	until
during such time	while
in respect of	for
in view of the fact	because
on the part of	by
subsequent to	after
under the provisions of	under
with a view to	to
it would appear that	apparently
it is probable that	probably
notwithstanding the fact	although
adequate number of	enough
excessive number of	too many
each and every	each
in the amount of $20	for $20

Word Doubles

If you're like most of us, in this hurry-up world, we tend to type too fast and proofread even faster. When we do, it's easy to overlook similar looking words that spell check doesn't pick up because they are spelled correctly, but their context is wrong.

These are called mixed doubles.

Watch these words because they can really change the meaning of your sentence.

Desert vs. Dessert

Desert has one [s] as in sand.

Dessert is a double sweet treat! (two s's)

Stripe vs. Strip

Can you imagine reading this embarrassing statement?

Henry used to stripe for the County Road's Department.

Henry used to strip for the Country Road's Department. Oh my!

Rhyme it to remember it:

Let it ripe if you want to stripe.

Let it rip if you want to strip.

Others:

Costumes/Customs

Discreet/Discrete

Faze/Phase

Her/Here

It's/Its

Loose instead of Lose

Not/Now

Of/For

Ravage/Ravish

Sent/Send

Spade/Spayed

To/Too

Totally instead of Totaling

You/Your

Your/You're

Word Switching

It's easy to incorrectly swap one word for another. We talked about eager vs. anxious and ensure vs. insure (page 65). If I wrote out all the commonly mistaken words, my list would be a mile long. So let me show you just a few that I come across all the time.

Commonly mistaken word usage:

accept: means to take it or agree to it
except: means exclude or leave out

affect: (when used as a verb) means to act upon or influence
effect: (when used as a noun) means result

aggravate: means to worsen
irritate: means to inflame

allude: means refer to indirectly
elude: means to evade

anonymous: means having an unknown or unacknowledged name
unanimous: means to share the same opinions or views

amiable: means generally pleasing
amicable: means friendly, goodwill

anticipate: means to give advance thought to
expect: means to look forward to

appraise: means to set a price on
apprise: means to inform

born: means produced by birth
borne: means carried

callous: means hardened
callus: means hard area on the skin

defuse: means to make less harmful
diffuse: means to pour out or spread widely

disburse: means to pay out
disperse: means to scatter

disinterested: means impartial
uninterested: means bored

equable: means free from variation or change
equitable: means fair

flounder: means to stumble awkwardly, clumsily; or, if you love to fish it means dinner!
founder: means to become disabled, collapse or break down or in the horse world it means laminitis (to go lame). It also means someone who established or started an organization or company.

forgo: means do without
forego: means go before

imply: means to suggest or to throw out a suggestion
infer: means to conclude or take in a suggestion

lightning: means that big electric bolt from the sky
lightening: means to lighten

loath: means unwilling to do something
loathe: means to dislike greatly

lose: is a verb and means the opposite of win or something misplaced.
loose: as an adjective means not fastened tightly, while loose as a verb means to free something.

raise: means to lift, something is being lifted
rise: means to get up

sediment: means material that settles to the bottom of a liquid
sentiment: means a thought, view, or attitude based on feeling or emotion

tortuous: means winding, crooked, full of turns
torturous: means painful

Writing Formally or Informally

Many writers find it hard to stay on course between using an informal (or chatty) style, and a very formal style. Are you writing a quick email to friends or family, or are you writing a letter of introduction to a new client? Are you writing a sales pitch or a request for proposal? The key to finding the right style for writing is to think about your intended reader and how you want them to portray you.

Whether you like your content to read in a formal style or informal style is totally up to you. It's okay to relax your writing style depending on the audience you want to attract. Just be sure to stay consistent with whatever style you choose.

Examples of Informal:

I loved that new book and couldn't put it down.

I'll be happy to give you a quote for my services.

She doesn't talk much.

Click Here for more info.

I think the author was trying to tell us what he felt.

Examples of Formal:

I enjoyed reading that new book and found it hard to put down.

I will be happy to provide you with a quote for services.

She is quite reserved in nature.

Please Click Here for more information.

It appears the author was attempting to convey his feelings.

BIBLIOGRAPHY

Many of these books I have religiously used as inspiration and reference in writing the 1st and 2nd Editions of *Grammar Done Right!*

References:

The American Heritage Dictionary. Boston: Houghton Mifflin, 2005

Chicago Manual of Style, 15th Edition. Chicago: University of Chicago Press, 2003

Elliott, R. *Painless Grammar.* New York: Barron's Educational Series, Inc., 1997

Fogarty, M. *Grammar Girl's Quick and Dirty Tips™.* New York: Henry Holt & Company, 2008

Garner, B. *Garner's Modern American Usage.* Oxford: Oxford University Press, 2003

McNichol, B. *Word Trippers: The Ultimate Source for Choosing the Perfect Word When It Really Matters,* ebook: Barbara McNichol Editorial, 2009 http://www.BarbaraMcNichol.com

O'Conner, P. *Woe Is I.* New York: Penguin Putnam, 1996

Sole, K. *What's the Rule?* California, Real World Publications, 2000

Strunk, Jr., W. and White, E.B. *The Elements of Style Fourth Edition.* Massachusetts: Longman Publishers, 2000

Webster's Standard American Style Manual. Massachusetts: Merriam-Webster Inc., Publishers, 1985

Zinsser, W. *On Writing Well, 30th Anniversary Edition,* New York: HarperCollins Publishers, 2006

Online Resources:

Cengage Learning, http://college.cengage.com

Fun-With-Words, http://www.fun-with-words.com

Merriam-Webster, http://merriam-webster.com

Your Dictionary, http://www.yourdictionary.com

ACKNOWLEDGMENTS

Thank you to all who cared enough about the rules of writing and grammar to purchase the 1st Edition of *Grammar Done Right!,* and to all who cared enough to comment, review, correct, support, and encourage me to keep producing grammar tips so this Revised and Expanded 2nd Edition could be completed.

INDEX

W

Y

ABOUT THE AUTHOR

Karen Reddick is a freelance book editor and creator of *Grammar Tips from The Red Pen Editor,* a weekly e-zine offering easy-to-understand grammar and writing tips. Her editing credits include numerous articles, e-books, booklets, web content, nonfiction business books, memoirs, self-help, how-to, historical; and, fiction mystery, sci-fi, fantasy, romance. She is the published author of *The A-Z Guide: The Best Ways to Work With a Virtual Assistant* and *Grammar Done Right! 1st Edition.* She's also written several industry articles, a children's book, short stories, and a novel.

Read the Editor's Blog at www.vandeservices.com/blog
Download her Grammar Done Right! Podcast on iTunes
Visit her websites at www.TheRedPenEditor.com • www.VandEservices.com

Printed in the United States
139814LV00002B/2/P